SKILL SHARPENERS

Third Edition

1

JUDY DeFILIPPO
CHARLES SKIDMORE

Longman

Judy DeFilippo supervises MATESL student teachers at Simmons College in Boston, Massachusetts. She is the author of *Lifeskills 1, 2,* and *3* and co-author of *Grammar Plus*.

Charles Skidmore is the principal of Arlington High School in Arlington, Massachusetts. He has taught and supervised the teaching of English as a Second Language for the past twenty-five years. He also serves as adjunct faculty in the Lynch School of Education at Boston College.

Pearson Education, 10 Bank Street, White Plains, NY 10606

Vice president, primary and secondary editorial: Ed Lamprich
Senior development editor: Virginia Bernard
Vice president, design and production: Rhea Banker
Director of editorial production: Linda Moser
Production supervisor: Melissa Leyva
Associate production editor: Laura Lazzaretti
Marketing managers: Alex Smith, Tania Saiz-Sousa
Senior manufacturing buyer: Dave Dickey
Cover design: Ann France
Cover photo: © Emma Lee/Life File/Getty Images
Text design adaptation: Tracey Munz Cataldo
Text composition: Laserwords
Text font: 11/19 Myriad Roman
Illustrations: Elizabeth Hazelton, Kathleen Todd, Andrew Lange
Photo credits: National Aeronautics and space Administration, p. 68;
    Library of Congress, pp. 76 and 105

ISBN: 0-13-192992-5
Printed in the United States of America
1 2 3 4 5 6 7 8 9 10–VHG–08 07 06 05 04

Introduction

The *Skill Sharpeners* series has been especially designed for students whose skills in standard English, especially those skills concerned with literacy, require strengthening. It is directed both toward students whose first language is not English and toward those who need additional practice in standard English grammar and vocabulary. By introducing basic skills tied to classroom subjects in a simple, easy-to-understand grammatical framework, the series helps to prepare these students for success in regular ("mainstream") academic subjects. By developing and reinforcing school and life survival skills, it helps build student confidence and self esteem.

Skills Sharpeners focuses on grammar practice and higher order thinking skills. It provides many content-area readings, biographies, opportunities for students to write, and practice in using formats similar to those of many standardized tests. The third edition updates the content of many pages. The central purpose of the series remains the same, however. *Skill Sharpeners* remains dedicated to helping your students sharpen their skills in all facets of English communication.

With English Language Learners, *Skill Sharpeners* supplements and complements any basic ESL text or series. With these students and with others, *Skill Sharpeners* can also be used to reteach and reinforce specific skills with which students are having or have had difficulty. In addition, it can be used to review and practice grammatical structures and to reinforce, expand, and enrich students' vocabularies.

The grammatical structures and the language objectives in *Skill Sharpeners* follow a systematic, small-step progression with many opportunities for practice, review, and reinforcement. Vocabulary and skill instruction is presented in the context of situations and concepts that have an immediate impact on students' daily lives. Themes and subject matter are directly related to curriculum areas. Reading and study skills are stressed in many pages, and writing skills are carefully developed, starting with single words and sentences and building gradually to paragraphs and stories in a structured, controlled composition sequence.

Skill Sharpeners is an ideal supplement for literature-based or sheltered English classrooms. *Skill Sharpeners* allows for direct teaching of grammar and language skills that most textbooks and novels do not supply. Students do not always intuitively grasp grammar and language rules. *Skill Sharpeners* has been designed to allow students a vehicle for continued practice in these areas.

Using the *Skill Sharpeners*

Because each page or pair of pages of the *Skill Sharpeners* is independent and self contained, the series lends itself to great flexibility of use. Teachers may pick and choose pages that fit the needs of particular students, or they may use the pages in sequential order. Most pages are self-explanatory, and all are easy to use, either in class or as homework assignments. Annotations at the bottom of each page identify the skill or skills being developed and suggest ways to prepare for, introduce, and present the exercise(s) on the page. In most cases, oral practice of the material is suggested before the student is asked to complete the page in writing. Teacher demonstration and student involvement and participation help build a foundation for completing the page successfully and learning the skill.

Skill Sharpeners is divided into thematic units. The first unit of each book is introductory. In *Skill Sharpeners 1*, this unit provides exercises to help students say and write their names and addresses and to familiarize them with basic classroom language, school deportment, the names of school areas and school personnel, and number names. In later books of the series, the first unit serves both to review some of the material taught in earlier books and to provide orientation to the series for students coming to it for the first time.

At the end of each of the *Skill Sharpeners* books is a review of vocabulary and an end-of-book test of grammatical and reading skills. The test, largely in multiple-choice format, not only assesses learning of the skills but also provides additional practice for other multiple-choice tests.

The Table of Contents in each book identifies the skills developed on each page. An Index at the end of the book provides an alphabetical list of language objectives. The language objectives are also displayed prominently at the top of each page.

Skill Sharpeners invites expansion! We encourage you to use them as a springboard and to add activities and exercises that build on those in the books to fill the needs of your own particular students. Used this way, the *Skill Sharpeners* can significantly help to build the confidence and skills that students need to be successful members of the community and successful achievers in subject-area classrooms.

Contents

Unit 1 What's Your Name?

Getting Started

Language Objectives
Answer questions about names. Ask and give personal information.

A Answer the questions. The first two are done for you.

1. What is her first name?

   Rita.

2. What is her last name?

   Gonzales.

3. Where is she from?

   _____

4. What is his first name?

   _____

5. What is his last name?

   _____

6. Where is he from?

   _____

My name is Rita Gonzales. I'm from Mexico.

My name is Dao Nguyen. I'm from Los Angeles.

B How about you? Answer these questions.

1. What is your first name?

   _____

2. What is your last name?

   _____

3. Where are you from?

   _____

DATA BANK			
he	is	last	what
her	first	name	where
his	from	she	

SKILL OBJECTIVE: Introducing oneself and others. Go over Part A orally with the class. Be sure they understand the concept of *first name* and *last name*. Help them to see how they can answer the questions by reading the "speech balloons." Encourage students to introduce themselves using the structures: "My name is ... I'm from ..." Check classmates' understanding by asking: "What's her/his first (last) name?" "Where's he/she from?" Introduce yourself using the same structures and follow-up questions. Be sure to write your name on the board. Briefly review the questions in Part B orally, then assign the page for independent written work.

1

Names, Addresses, and Numbers

Language Objectives
Provide personal information.
Agree or disagree about information.

A Answer the questions.

1. What is her first name? _____

2. What is her last name? _____

3. What is her address? _____

4. What is her zip code? _____

5. What is her telephone number? _____

Easy-Air

NAME · NOMBRE · NOM
Mary Johnson
ADDRESS · DIRECCION · ADRESSE
30 Tower Road
CITY · CIUDAD · VILLE   STATE · ESTADO · PROVINCIA · ETAT
Sunnyvale   California
TELEPHONE · TELEFONO
TELEPHONE   ZIP CODE · ZONA POSTAL · CODE POSTAL
245-5163   94087

B Answer the questions. The first two are done for you.

1. Is his first name Peter? _Yes, it is._

2. Is his last name Smith? _No, it isn't._

3. What is his phone number? _____

4. Is his zip code 02117? _____

5. Is her last name Linda? _____

6. What is her library card number? _____

7. What is her phone number? _____

8. What is her address? _____

Easy-Air

NAME · NOMBRE · NOM
Peter Carlson
ADDRESS · DIRECCION · ADRESSE
22 Hunt St.
CITY · CIUDAD · VILLE   STATE · ESTADO · PROVINCIA · ETAT
Quincy   Mass.
TELEPHONE · TELEFONO
TELEPHONE   ZIP CODE · ZONA POSTAL · CODE POSTAL
926-3586   02170

Linda Sutton
38 Whitcome Ave.   Tel.
Chicago, IL.   949-2901
is entitled to borrow books from the
READING PUBLIC LIBRARY
and is responsible for all use made of this card WHICH
MUST BE PRESENTED each time a book is borrowed.

1381   № 7381

C Write the information on your card.

IDENTIFICATION

Name _____

Street _____

City _____

State _____ Zip _____

Telephone _____

SKILL OBJECTIVE: Discussing address labels, library cards, ID cards. Teach or review the vocabulary used on these forms. *Part A:* Practice reading the first label with the class. *Part B:* Have a student read the Peter Carlson label aloud. Ask: "What state does Peter live in?" Discuss how state names are abbreviated. Have students answer the questions orally. *Part C:* Let volunteers dictate their addresses and phone numbers to the rest of the class. Write each address and phone number on the board so the students can correct their writing. Then assign the page for independent written work.

Classroom Language

Look at the pictures. Fill in the words from the Data Bank below.
The first one is done for you.

1. Please ____sit____ down.

2. _____ to this.

3. _____ at this.

4. _____ with a _____.

5. _____ your hand.

6. _____ your books.

7. _____ your books.

8. _____ on the _____.

DATA BANK

Look at this.	Work with a partner.
Open your books.	Close your books.
~~Please sit down.~~	Write on the board.
Raise your hand.	Listen to this.

SKILL OBJECTIVE: Understanding classroom commands. Introduce each command by reading the sentence and pointing to the picture. Then have the students act out the correct response as you repeat the commands several times, first in sequence and then in random order. Keep the pace lively during this activity. If appropriate, have students give commands to each other. As the final activity, assign this page for independent written work. If necessary, students may refer to the Data Bank as they fill in the missing words.

3

Things to Remember

Language Objective
Learn school rules.

Look at the pictures. Fill in the words from the Data Bank below. The first one is done for you.

1. _____Walk_____ in the hall.

2. Don't _____ in the hall.

3. Be on _____ for class.

4. Don't come _____.

5. _____ your hand.

6. Don't _____ out in class.

7. Pay _____ to your teacher.

8. Don't _____ in class.

9. Do your _____.

10. Don't chew _____.

DATA BANK

Be on time for class.	Raise your hand.	Don't chew gum.
Pay attention to your teacher.	Don't whisper in class.	Don't come late.
~~Walk in the hall.~~	Don't run in the hall.	Don't shout out in class.
Do your homework.		

SKILL OBJECTIVE: Understanding school rules. Review these school rules with the class, reading each directive aloud and studying the pictures together. Act out one of the misdemeanors. (Example: coming late to class.) Let the class give the rule that points out what you have done wrong ("Don't come late.") and the rule that tells what you should do ("Be on time."). Let volunteers act out the other misdemeanors; have the class correct them by giving the appropriate rule(s). Then assign the page for independent written work.

Which Way?

Look at the pictures. Write the correct word from the Data Bank below. The first one is done for you.

Language Objective
Understand and use prepositions and direction words.

 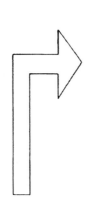  

1. __left__   2. _____   3. _____   4. _____

5. _____   6. _____   7. _____   8. _____

DATA BANK			
down	~~left~~	on	right
in	off	out	up

SKILL OBJECTIVE: Understanding direction words. Teach and practice *left/right* by giving students "marching" directions: "Turn left. Walk 1, 2, 3. Turn right," etc. To practice *up/down*, tell the class: "Point up. Point down. Point right." Steadily increase the speed of these directions. Help the class name the picture pairs on this page, then ask for names in random order, "Number 7. What is it?" Have the class read the prepositions in the Data Bank and find the matching pictures. Assign the page for independent written work.

At School

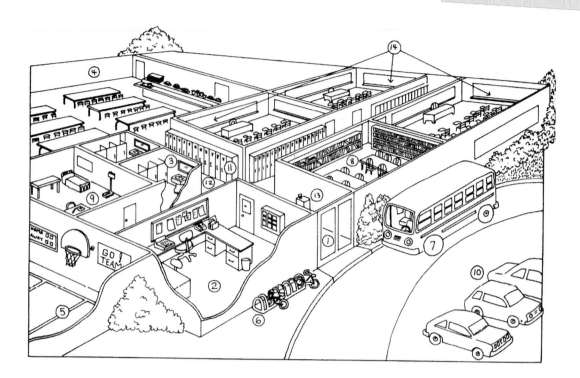

Find the number in the picture. Write the word on the line. The first one is done for you.

1. _____entrance_____

2. _____

3. _____

4. _____

5. _____

6. _____

7. _____

8. _____

9. _____

10. _____

11. _____

12. _____

13. _____

14. _____

DATA BANK

bathroom	bike rack	classrooms	hallway
library	lockers	cafeteria	nurse's office
office	parking lot	gym	school bus
water fountain	~~entrance~~		

SKILL OBJECTIVES: Naming school locations; reading a map. Help students identify the fourteen locations numbered on the school map. Provide practice with the terms by asking:"Where is the (office)? *(It's number 2.)* Do we have an (office) in our school? What is number …? Where do we (eat lunch, leave our bikes)?" Adjust the time spent on this oral activity to the needs and skill level of your students. Assign the page for independent written work. Students may refer to the Data Bank as needed.

People and Places at School

A Who is she? Who is he? Write the words. The first one is done for you.

1. ___principal___

2. _____

3. _____

4. _____

5. _____

6. _____

DATA BANK
bus driver   gym teacher   librarian   math teacher   nurse   ~~principal~~

B Where is he? Where is she? Write the words. The first one is done for you.

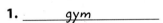

1. ___gym___

2. _____

3. _____

4. _____

5. _____

6. _____

DATA BANK
classroom   library   nurse's office   hallway   cafeteria   ~~gym~~

SKILL OBJECTIVE: Naming school personnel and school locations. Teach or review the vocabulary highlighted on the page. Relate the terms to your school by asking:" Who is the (principal) in our school? Who is your (math teacher)? Where is the (water fountain)?" Go over both parts of the page orally, adjusting the amount of oral practice to the needs of your students. Then assign the page for independent written work.

Number Names

0	1	2	3	4	5	6	7	8	9	10
zero	one	two	three	four	five	six	seven	eight	nine	ten

11	12	13	14	15	16	17
eleven	twelve	thirteen	fourteen	fifteen	sixteen	seventeen

18	19	20	21	30	40	50	60
eighteen	nineteen	twenty	twenty-one	thirty	forty	fifty	sixty

70	80	90	100	101	1,000
seventy	eighty	ninety	one hundred	one hundred one	one thousand

A Write the number names.

1 _____one_____

19 _____

5 _____

300 _____

20 _____

90 _____

3 _____

17 _____

201 _____

220 _____

88 _____

308 _____

60,000 _____

70 _____

33 _____

B Write the numbers.

twenty-seven _____27_____

forty-three _____

nine _____

one hundred five _____

C Write the number names in the boxes.

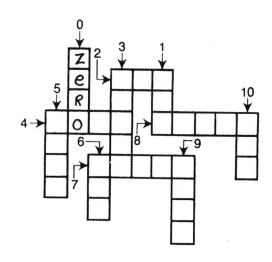

SKILL OBJECTIVE: Naming numbers 1–10,000. Use any or all of the following introductory activities, depending on the needs of the students. 1. Have students count from 1 to 100, either in chorus or in sequence, going around the room. If possible, display a number chart. 2. Write random numbers on the board for volunteers to name. 3. Name a number from 1 to 10,000 and have students write the numeral at their desks. Write the answer on the board so that students can immediately check and correct their work. Then review the directions and assign the page for independent written work.

8

What Time Is It?

Language Objective
Tell time.

Look at the clocks. Write the sentences. The first one is done for you.

1. ___It's one o'clock.___

2. _____

3. _____

4. _____

5. _____

6. _____

7. _____

8. _____

9. _____

10. _____

11. _____

12. _____

SKILL OBJECTIVE: Telling time on the hour. Go over the page as an oral group activity. First, have students lants read the twelve clocks in sequence. Then ask, "What time is it?" and name the clocks in random order. After sufficient oral practice, assign the page for independent written work.

Matching Times

Write the letter of the matching clock. The first one is done for you.

1. It's six o'clock. ___c___ a. 3:00

2. It's twelve o'clock. _____ b. 9:00

3. It's three o'clock. _____ c. 6:00

4. It's seven o'clock. _____ d. 5:00

5. It's four o'clock. _____ e. 7:00

6. It's nine o'clock. _____ f. 12:00

7. It's five o'clock. _____ g. 10:00

8. It's ten o'clock. _____ h. 1:00

9. It's one o'clock. _____ i. 4:00

10. It's two o'clock. _____ j. 11:00

11. It's eleven o'clock. _____ k. 2:00

12. It's eight o'clock. _____ l. 8:00

SKILL OBJECTIVE: Telling time on the hour. Draw attention to the clocks on the right side of the page. Name a clock by its letter, and ask a student to tell the time. Give all students a chance to respond at least once to the question, "What time is it?" For further practice, state a time ("It's ten o'clock.") and have students identify, by letter, the correct clock. After sufficient practice, assign this page for independent work.

Where Is It?

Language Objective
Locate objects.

Where's the window?

It's on the left.

Learn the names of the things in the picture. Then answer the questions. The first one is done for you.

1. Where's the bookcase?   It's on the left.

2. Where's the door?   _____

3. Where's the board?   _____

4. Where's the clock?   _____

5. Where's the calendar?   _____

6. Where's the pencil sharpener?   _____

7. Where's the eraser?   _____

8. Where's the waste-paper basket?   _____

DATA BANK	
on the left	on the right

SKILL OBJECTIVES: Naming classroom furniture and objects; distinguishing left and right. Review the concept of *left* and *right*.
Ask, "Raise your right hand, your left hand. Point to the right, to the left," etc. Go over the vocabulary in the picture and have students point to the same items in your classroom. Ask about these items in your room, "Where's the (window)?" and elicit the response, "It's on the (right)." Go through the eight questions orally with the class, then assign the page for independent written work.

Tell When, Tell Where

Language Objectives
Name the days of the week.
Respond to _where/when_ questions.

Sunday

Monday

The Days of the Week

Sunday	Monday	Tuesday	Wednesday	Thursday	Friday	Saturday
SUN	MON	TUES	WED	THURS	FRI	SAT
S	M	T	W	T or TH	F	S

Tuesday

When

**Look at the pictures. Then answer the questions.
The first one is done for you.**

1. When is Mike at the park? _____On Sunday._____

2. When is Mike in the hallway? _____

3. When is Mike at the movies? _____

4. When is Mike at the water fountain? _____

5. When is Mike in the cafeteria? _____

6. When is Mike at the nurse's office? _____

7. When is Mike in the library? _____

Wednesday

Where

**Look at the pictures again. Then answer the questions.
The first one is done for you.**

Thursday

1. Where is Mike on Monday? _____In the library._____

2. Where is Mike on Wednesday? _____

3. Where is Mike on Saturday? _____

4. Where is Mike on Friday? _____

5. Where is Mike on Tuesday? _____

6. Where is Mike on Thursday? _____

7. Where is Mike on Sunday? _____

Friday

Saturday

SKILL OBJECTIVES: Naming the days of the week; using pictures to answer questions. Teach or review the days of the week. If possible let students examine several calendars and note the different abbreviations used. Point out that in the United States, Sunday is considered the first day of the week. (In many countries, calendars show the week starting with Monday.) Do several examples from both the "When" part and the "Where" part orally with the class, showing how the pictures are used to provide the answers. Then assign the page for independent written work.

Reading a Calendar

Language Objectives
Use ordinal numbers for dates.
Respond to <u>when</u> questions.

SEPTEMBER

S	M	T	W	TH	F	S
		1	2	3	4	5 _Family party_
6	7	8	9 _First day of class_	10	11	12
13	14	15	16	17	18	19
20	21 _Don's birthday_	22	23 _Soccer game_	24	25	26 _Sue's birthday_
27	28	29 _Doctor's appointment_	30			

A Look at the calendar and the Data Bank. Answer the questions using words from the Data Bank. The first one is done for you.

1. When is the first day of class?   It's September ninth.

2. When is the family party?   _____

3. When is the soccer game?   _____

4. When is Don's birthday?   _____

5. When is Sue's birthday?   _____

6. When is the doctor's appointment?   _____

DATA BANK

1	first	1st	11	eleventh	11th	21	twenty-first	21st
2	second	2nd	12	twelfth	12th	22	twenty-second	22nd
3	third	3rd	13	thirteenth	13th	23	twenty-third	23rd
4	fourth	4th	14	fourteenth	14th	24	twenty-fourth	24th
5	fifth	5th	15	fifteenth	15th	25	twenty-fifth	25th
6	sixth	6th	16	sixteenth	16th	26	twenty-sixth	26th
7	seventh	7th	17	seventeenth	17th	27	twenty-seventh	27th
8	eighth	8th	18	eighteenth	18th	28	twenty-eighth	28th
9	ninth	9th	19	nineteenth	19th	29	twenty-ninth	29th
10	tenth	10th	20	twentieth	20th	30	thirtieth	30th

B Fill in more boxes on the calendar. Show your calendar to a classmate and ask and answer questions like the ones above.

The Months of the Year

Language Objectives
Name the months of the year. Use ordinal numbers as dates. Use the adverbs _before_ and _after_ correctly.

Look at the calendar.

JANUARY						
S	M	T	W	T	F	S
1	2	3	4	5	6	7
8	9	10	11	12	13	14
15	16	17	18	19	20	21
22	23	24	25	26	27	28
29	30	31				

FEBRUARY						
S	M	T	W	T	F	S
			1	2	3	4
5	6	7	8	9	10	11
12	13	14	15	16	17	18
19	20	21	22	23	24	25
26	27	28	29			

MARCH						
S	M	T	W	T	F	S
				1	2	3
4	5	6	7	8	9	10
11	12	13	14	15	16	17
18	19	20	21	22	23	24
25	26	27	28	29	30	31

APRIL						
S	M	T	W	T	F	S
1	2	3	4	5	6	7
8	9	10	11	12	13	14
15	16	17	18	19	20	21
22	23	24	25	26	27	28
29	30					

MAY						
S	M	T	W	T	F	S
		1	2	3	4	5
6	7	8	9	10	11	12
13	14	15	16	17	18	19
20	21	22	23	24	25	26
27	28	29	30	31		

JUNE						
S	M	T	W	T	F	S
					1	2
3	4	5	6	7	8	9
10	11	12	13	14	15	16
17	18	19	20	21	22	23
24	25	26	27	28	29	30

JULY						
S	M	T	W	T	F	S
1	2	3	4	5	6	7
8	9	10	11	12	13	14
15	16	17	18	19	20	21
22	23	24	25	26	27	28
29	30	31				

AUGUST						
S	M	T	W	T	F	S
			1	2	3	4
5	6	7	8	9	10	11
12	13	14	15	16	17	18
19	20	21	22	23	24	25
26	27	28	29	30	31	

SEPTEMBER						
S	M	T	W	T	F	S
						1
2	3	4	5	6	7	8
9	10	11	12	13	14	15
16	17	18	19	20	21	22
23	24	25	26	27	28	29
30						

OCTOBER						
S	M	T	W	T	F	S
	1	2	3	4	5	6
7	8	9	10	11	12	13
14	15	16	17	18	19	20
21	22	23	24	25	26	27
28	29	30	31			

NOVEMBER						
S	M	T	W	T	F	S
				1	2	3
4	5	6	7	8	9	10
11	12	13	14	15	16	17
18	19	20	21	22	23	24
25	26	27	28	29	30	

DECEMBER						
S	M	T	W	T	F	S
						1
2	3	4	5	6	7	8
9	10	11	12	13	14	15
16	17	18	19	20	21	22
23	24	25	26	27	28	29
30	31					

A Complete each sentence with the correct month. The first one is done for you.

1. May is before _June._
2. December is after _____.
3. March is before _____.
4. August is after _____.
5. October is after _____.
6. January is before _____.

> **Learn to Say Dates**
>
> We write: December 20.
> We say: "December twentieth."
>
> We write: 2005
> We say: "two thousand five."
>
> Your teacher can help you to say other dates.

B We can write dates two ways: 6/9/05 and June 9, 2005. The month always comes first. "6" stands for June because June is the sixth month in the year. In your notebook, write each date the other way.

1. April 4, 2004
2. 7/1/88
3. January 24, 1995
4. 2/9/07
5. May 17, 2005
6. 10/12/00
7. November 8, 1990
8. 3/13/06
9. 8/30/04
10. September 14, 2005
11. 12/25/93
12. June 2, 1991

SKILL OBJECTIVES: Reading a calendar, naming the months; understanding _before_ and _after_. _Part A:_ Teach/review the names of the months. Give twelve students cards with the name of a month on each card; have them read their cards and line up in order (January, February, March, etc.). Repeat with other students. Teach or review _before_ and _after_. Ask, "What month is before (June)? What month is after (March)? Is July after August?" etc. _Part B:_ On the board, explain the two ways of writing dates given on the page. Do the first three or four items orally before assigning the page for independent written work.

May I?

A Read these dialogues with a classmate.

 May I go to the bathroom, please?

Yes, you may.

 May I open the window, please?

No, you may not.

B Look at the pictures. Write the questions.

erase the board

1. __May I erase the board, please?__

see the nurse

2. _____

go to the library

3. _____

sharpen my pencil

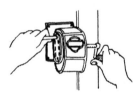

4. _____

call home

5. _____

go to the office

6. _____

SKILL OBJECTIVE: Asking permission. Teach or review the vocabulary on the page. Let students ask one another permission to go places and to do things. They should use the forms, "May I . . ., please?" and "Yes, you may./No, you may not." Students need not restrict themselves to the places and actions pictured. Be sure all students have a chance to participate in this oral practice. Assign the page for independent written work.

Talking About Feelings

A Look at the pictures. Talk about each word.

confused

tired   happy   sad   sick   nervous

B Write a dialogue for each picture. The first two are done for you. Use them as examples.

1. A: How do you feel?
   B: I feel confused.
   A: Maybe I can help.
   B: Thanks.

2. A: How are you?
   B: Very happy!
   A: What happened?
   B: I passed my test.

3. _____
   _____
   _____
   _____

4. _____
   _____
   _____
   _____

5. _____
   _____
   _____
   _____

6. _____
   _____
   _____
   _____

C Now practice your dialogues with a classmate.

SKILL OBJECTIVES: Describing feelings; writing short dialogues. Teach or review the vocabulary highlighted on this page.
Part A: Have the class mime the emotions illustrated at the top of the page. Each time ask, "What's the matter?" or "How do you feel?" The class will respond, "I/We feel . . ." Then encourage students to ask one another these questions and respond as they choose. *Part B:* On the board, do items 1 and 2 together so that students understand how to write the dialogue. Discuss other possible responses (for example, "That's too bad," "I'm sorry" for item 1). Then assign the page for independent written work.

Class Rules

Look at the chalkboard.

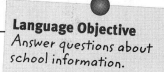
GOOD MORNING !

THIS IS MRS. CHACON'S ENGLISH 1 CLASS AT ALLSTON HIGH SCHOOL.

TODAY IS WEDNESDAY , SEPTEMBER 9.

CLASS RULES

1. BE ON TIME FOR CLASS.
2. RAISE YOUR HAND TO ANSWER A QUESTION.
3. PAY ATTENTION TO YOUR TEACHER.
4. LISTEN.
5. DO YOUR HOMEWORK.

Answer the questions. Fill in the circle. The first one is done for you.

1. What day is it?   ⓐ ⓑ ●
  a. Monday
  b. Tuesday
  c. Wednesday

2. What is the date?   ⓐ ⓑ ⓒ
  a. September 3
  b. September 9
  c. September 4

3. What is the name of the high school?   ⓐ ⓑ ⓒ
  a. Arlington High School
  b. Austin High School
  c. Allston High School

4. Who is the teacher?   ⓐ ⓑ ⓒ
  a. Mrs. Johnson
  b. Mr. Allston
  c. Mrs. Chacon

5. What is *not* a rule in Mrs. Chacon's class?   ⓐ ⓑ ⓒ
  a. Raise your hand to answer a question.
  b. Pay attention to the teacher.
  c. Shout out in class.

6. What is the name of the class?   ⓐ ⓑ ⓒ
  a. English 1
  b. Allston
  c. French

SKILL OBJECTIVE: Reading rules and information. Review vocabulary from pages 3 and 4 if necessary. Call on volunteers to read the message on the "chalkboard" at the top of the page. Ask students questions about the message, for example, "What day is it? What's the date?" Do questions 1 and 2 together. Emphasize that students are to choose only one answer for each question. Show them how to fill in the circles to indicate their answers. Then assign the page for independent work. Note: This format is used here and elsewhere to give students practice in one kind of standardized test question setup.

Language Objective
Name articles of clothing.

 1.   2.   3.   4.   5.   6.

 7.   8.   9.   10.   11.   12.

 13.   14.   15.   16.   17.   18.

Find the picture. Write the sentence. The first one is done for you.

1. _It's a hat._
2. _____
3. _____
4. _____
5. _____
6. _____
7. _____
8. _____
9. _____

10. _____
11. _____
12. _____
13. _____
14. _____
15. _____
16. _____
17. _____
18. _____

DATA BANK

pair of shorts	shirt	pair of socks	scarf	~~hat~~
tie	raincoat	pair of glasses	jacket	dress
pair of jeans	belt	pair of boots	sweater	skirt
blouse	bathrobe	pair of sneakers		

SKILL OBJECTIVE: Naming articles of clothing. Teach or review the clothing vocabulary highlighted on this page. Call attention to the Data Bank and point out in particular the items referred to as "a pair of ..." Have students quiz each other on the clothing vocabulary in a chain conversation: Student A, "What's number (six)?" Student B, "It's a (raincoat)." (To Student C): "What's number (eleven)?" etc. After sufficient oral practice, assign the page as independent written work.

What Are They Wearing?

Language Objective
Describe what people are wearing.

Write what each person is wearing. The first one is done for you.

1. She is wearing a T-shirt and a pair of shorts.

2. _____

3. _____

4. _____

5. _____

6. _____

7. _____

8. _____

SKILL OBJECTIVES: Discussing clothes; writing descriptions. Review clothing vocabulary by making a statement about what you are wearing. ("I am wearing a blouse, a skirt, and a sweater.") Ask students, "What are you wearing?" "What is (Maria) wearing?" Have students read the description written next to the first picture. In each description, students should list two items the person is wearing. Have the class do all or some of the page orally before you assign it as independent written work. Listen for correct use of the pronouns *he* and *she*.

Counting American Money

Language Objectives
Name coins and currency.
Count money.

A How much is it worth? Write the words. The first one is done for you.

| a penny | a nickel | a dime | a quarter |

one cent _____ _____ _____

| $1.00 | $5.00 | $10.00 | $20.00 |

one dollar _____ _____ _____

a quarter twenty-five cents 25¢	a dime ten cents 10¢	a penny one cent 1¢	a nickel five cents 5¢
ten dollars $10.00	twenty dollars $20.00	five dollars $5.00	one dollar $1.00

B How much money do you have? Write the numbers. The first one is done for you.

1. _____ $1.45

2. _____

3. _____

C Write the amount. The first one is done for you.

1. $2.63 _two dollars and sixty-three cents_

2. $5.05 _____

3. $7.99 _____

4. $20.22 _____

SKILL OBJECTIVES: Counting money; reading and writing prices. Bring coins and bills to class. Have students practice counting money, reporting and writing each amount as a number and a phrase. *Part A:* Have the class identify the value of each coin, then let students write the answers. Assign Part B, then correct and discuss as a class. *Part C:* Have students read the prices aloud. Note that $2.63 is read as "two sixty-three," but written as *two dollars and sixty-three cents*.

Money Problems

Answer these questions.

1. Ben has a penny, two dimes, three nickels, a quarter, and a five dollar bill. How much money is this?

    _____

2. Nadia is buying a scarf. It is eight dollars and fifty cents. She has a ten dollar bill. How much is Nadia's change?

    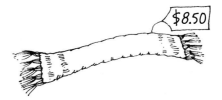

    _____

3. A shoe store is having a sale. Mrs. Yakos is buying two pairs of sneakers. How much money is that?

    _____

4. Look at the sweater, the pair of jeans, and the pair of boots. Willie has two twenty dollar bills.

    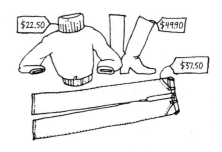

    Can he buy the sweater, jeans, and boots? _____

    Can he buy the sweater and the jeans? _____

    Can he buy the jeans? _____

    How much is his change? _____

5. This is the Baxter family. They are eating chicken dinners. Each dinner is $5.00. How much is the bill?

    _____

6. James and June are twins. It's their birthday today. Their father and mother are giving them $100.00. The twins are dividing the money evenly. How much is June's present?

    _____

SKILL OBJECTIVES: Understanding math language and money transactions. Bring in real coins and bills or use realistic "play money." Put price tags on classroom objects. Let students role-play salesperson and customer: selecting items, computing the bill, deciding if it is affordable, and paying and receiving change. Supervise closely, or and allow independent pair practice, depending on the skill level of your group. Discuss the page to decide which math process must be used to solve each problem, then assign for independent work.

Categories

A Circle the word that doesn't belong. The first one is done for you.

1. Bob   Paul   (Mary)   Mario

2. five   seven   first   ten

3. street   avenue   road   skirt

4. Monday   Thursday   Friday   March

5. red   yes   blue   yellow

6. blouse   shoes   boots   sandals

7. teacher   library   principal   nurse

8. wearing   looking   sitting   morning

9. she   they   his   I

10. brown   blouse   blue   pink

B Add one word which belongs in the category. The first one is done for you.

1. slippers   sneakers   boots   *sandals*

2. tennis   baseball   football   _____

3. slacks   trousers   jeans   _____

4. she   he   it   _____

5. February   October   July   _____

6. New York   Texas   California   _____

7. sister   father   mother   _____

8. zip code   street   name   _____

C Study the picture below as long as you wish. When you think you can remember the names of all or most of the items, close the book. In your notebook, write the names of the items you remember. There are eight items. Then compare your list with the picture.

This and That

Language Objectives
Answer a question in the negative. Distinguish between demonstrative adjectives. Use the singular possessive form.

A Answer the questions by changing *this* to *that*.

1. Is this your sweater? No, _____that_____ is my sweater.

2. Is this your belt? No, _____ is my belt.

3. Is this your scarf? No, _____ is my scarf.

4. Is this your jacket? No, _____ is my jacket.

5. Is this your bathrobe? No, _____ is my bathrobe.

B Answer the questions by changing *my* to *your*.

1. Is this your blouse? No, this is _____my_____ blouse.

2. Is this your tie? No, this is _____ tie.

3. Is this your skirt? No, this is _____ skirt.

4. Is this your shoe? No, this is _____ shoe.

5. Is this your sock? No, this is _____ sock.

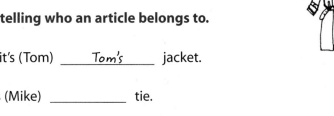

C Answer the questions by telling who an article belongs to.

1. Is that Bill's jacket? No, it's (Tom) _____Tom's_____ jacket.

2. Is this Binh's tie? No, it's (Mike) _____ tie.

3. Is this Rosa's skirt? No. it's (Maria) _____ skirt.

4. Is that Eliot's coat? No, it's (Nelson) _____ coat.

5. Is that Sabrina's belt? No, it's (Tiffany) _____ belt.

6. Is this Andrew's bathrobe? No, it's (Pedro) _____ bathrobe.

7. Is this Sally's dress? No, it's (Jackie) _____ dress.

8. Is this Susan's hat? No, it's (Kate) _____ hat.

SKILL OBJECTIVES: Answering a question in the negative; using the correct form of the demonstrative adjectives *this* and *that*; using the singular possessive form. *Part A:* Tell students that you want to teach them how to say *no* to a question. Show that the adjectives *this* and *that* denote distance; *this* is something near while *that* is something more distant. Exaggerate the difference as you act them out for students. *Part B:* Continue practicing the difference between *this* and *that* and call students' attention in the change from *you* to *my*. *Part C:* Make students aware of the possessive singular form as they finish with *this* and *that* questions.

The Four Seasons

Language Objective
Relate clothing to seasons of the year.

Read the paragraph.

Many parts of the United States have four very different seasons. Winter is the cold season from December to March. Spring is the warm and rainy season. It lasts from March until June. Summer is the hot time of the year from June until September. The autumn or fall is the cool time of year. It is from September until December.

A Look at the pictures. Each shows one season. Write the name of the season under each picture.

   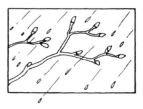

_____ _____ _____ _____

B Read each description and answer the question after it.

1. Frannie is wearing a hat, gloves, a big coat, and boots.

What season is it? _____

2. Jack is outside. He is wearing shorts and a T-shirt. He's not wearing shoes.

What season is it? _____

3. Maria is going to a party. She puts on a light jacket and takes her umbrella.

What season is it? _____

4. Raul is wearing a shirt and sweater and long pants. He is going to a football game.

What season is it? _____

C Tell what season each month is in.

1. January _____ **5.** February _____

2. July _____ **6.** November _____

3. October _____ **7.** August _____

4. May _____ **8.** April _____

SKILL OBJECTIVES: Reading for details; making inferences. Discuss seasons with the class. Ask, "What season is it now?" Establish that in many countries there are four distinct seasons. Then read the paragraph aloud. Point out that it refers to "many parts of the United States," particularly the northern states. (States and other countries closer to the Equator have only two seasons—a wet season and a dry season.) Also point out that in the southern hemisphere the seasons are reversed. *Part A:* Do the first picture with the class. Ask why they think the picture shows fall. Let them do the other pictures. *Part B:* Do the first question orally. Let them complete the others independently. *Part C:* Do several questions with the class, then let them complete the others independently.

Asking Questions

Who, What, Where, and *When* are words you use to start a question.

- **Who** asks about a person → John, my friends, the girls

- **What** asks about a thing → the desk, my books, the houses

- **Where** asks about a place → at school, in the house, in Mexico

- **When** asks about a time → at 3:00, in January, on Monday

A   Match the questions to the answers. Write the letter on the line. The first one is done for you.

1. Who is your teacher? _____d_____   **a.** It's at 9:00.

2. Where is Mike? _____   **b.** He's my friend, Jos.

3. What is Paul wearing? _____   **c.** It's in France.

4. When is the party? _____   **d.** Mrs. Chacon is my teacher.

5. Who is that boy? _____   **e.** It's in December.

6. Where is Paris? _____   **f.** He's wearing a blue sweater.

7. When is Christmas? _____   **g.** She's wearing a red dress.

8. What is Mary wearing? _____   **h.** He's in the cafeteria.

B   Now you try. Look at the Data Bank below. Find a question for each answer. The first one is done for you.

1. _Where is Susan?_ _____   She's at the nurse's office.

2. _____ ?   Mr. Tyson is my teacher.

3. _____ ?   It's in September.

4. _____ ?   She's wearing a green dress.

5. _____ ?   It's at 10:00.

6. _____ ?   It's in the United States.

DATA BANK	
~~Where is Susan?~~	When is your English class?
Where is New York?	What is Susan wearing?
Who is your teacher?	When is Labor Day?

SKILL OBJECTIVE: Asking and writing *wh-* questions. Discuss the question words at the top of the page and give an example of a question or two using each one. *Part A:* Do the first two matching questions together to be sure that students understand that they are to write the letter of the matching answer next to each question. *Part B:* Call attention to the Data Bank. Work through the items orally before assigning the page for independent or pair work.

Flags with Stars

Read the article about flags.

Every country has a flag. A flag is designed to give a message about a country. Flags may have stripes, circles, crescents, objects, and stars.

The flag of the United States has fifty stars on it. It has more stars than any other country's flag. Every star represents a state. The flag of Ghana has one black star. Some people say this black star means that Ghana was the first African country to become independent. The flag of Australia has a group of five stars and one large star separate from them. The five stars are in the shape of a constellation called the Southern Cross. The Southern Cross is seen only in countries far south of the Equator. People in Australia can see the Southern Cross. The big star in the flag stands for Australia itself.

United States

Ghana

Australia

A **Now answer the following questions in your notebook.**

1. How are the flags of Australia and the United States similar?

2. How many stars are in the flag of the United States?

3. Which country's flag has stars in the shape of a constellation?

4. Which country's flag has more stars than any other country's flag?

5. What does the big star on Ghana's flag stand for?

6. What is the purpose of a flag?

B **Write how many stars each country's flag has. Use an atlas, an encyclopedia, or the Internet to find the answers.**

Senegal	Honduras	Singapore	Morocco	Panama
1 star				

C **Name other flags that have stars on them. Use an encyclopedia or the Internet to find your answer.**

A Write the sentence. The first two are done for you.

1. It's three o'clock.

2. It's a quarter to six.

3. _____

4. _____

5. _____

6. _____

7. _____

8. _____

9. _____

10. _____

11. _____

12. _____

B Look at the signs and answer the questions. The first two are done for you.

LACY'S SHOES	**U.S. POST OFFICE**	**FIRST BANK**
Hours	*Hours*	*Hours*
Monday–Saturday 9:30 AM to 9:30 PM Sunday: 12:00 PM–6:00 PM	Monday–Friday 8:00 AM to 6:00 PM Saturday: 8:00 AM–12:00 PM	Monday–Friday 8:30 to 3:30 Saturday: 9–12

1. What are Lacy's hours on Tuesday?   9:30 a.m.–9:30 p.m.

2. Is Lacy's open on Sunday?   Yes, it is.

3. What are the hours at the Post Office on Monday?   _____

4. When is the Post Office open on Saturday?   _____

5. What are the bank's hours on Thursday?   _____

6. Is the bank open on Saturday?   _____

SKILL OBJECTIVES: Telling time; reading signs. Review telling time on the hour. If possible, use a practice clock with movable hands to teach (or review) "quarter to …,""quarter past …," and "half past …." *Part A:* Work through part or all of the items in an oral group exercise before assigning them for independent written work. *Part B:* Read the signs aloud. Have students read "12:00–6:00" as "from twelve to six." Discuss the need for this kind of information. Have pairs of students ask each other the six questions and make up questions of their own. Then assign the page for independent written work.

Barrington Bus Company

BARRINGTON BUS COMPANY

★ DAILY SERVICE ★

Tickets:
One way—$8.00
Round trip—$15.00

—— BARRINGTON TO PLYMOUTH ——	
Leaves Barrington	Arrives Plymouth
6:30 a.m.	8:30 a.m.
11:30 a.m.	1:30 p.m.
4:30 a.m.	6:30 p.m.

—— PLYMOUTH TO BARRINGTON ——	
Leaves Plymouth	Arrives Barrington
9:00 a.m.	11:00 a.m.
2:00 p.m.	4:00 p.m.
7:00 p.m.	9:00 p.m.

Look at the bus schedule. Then write the answer in the blank space. The first one is done for you.

1. The first bus leaves Barrington at ___6:30 a.m.___ and arrives in Plymouth at _____.

2. The bus trip from Barrington to Plymouth is _____ hours.

3. The 11:30 a.m. bus arrives in Plymouth at _____.

4. There are _____ morning trips to Plymouth.

5. A one-way ticket from Barrington to Plymouth is $ _____.

6. The last bus leaves Barrington at _____.

7. The first bus leaves Plymouth at _____ and arrives in Barrington at _____.

8. There are _____ bus trips from Plymouth to Barrington every day.

9. A round-trip ticket (from Barrington to Barrington) is $ _____.

10. You arrive in Plymouth at 8:30 a.m. and spend all day there with a friend. The last bus you can take home to Barrington leaves at _____.

SKILL OBJECTIVE: Reading a bus schedule. Teach/review vocabulary on the bus schedule. Ask questions about bus times and ticket prices. Help students to examine the schedule to find the answers. When they are comfortable with this chart-reading skill, have them look at the sentences below the schedule. Point out that some of the sentences have two blank spaces, some have only one. Demonstrate how to use the schedule to find the answer. Have the class decide on the correct answer for the second blank in item 1. Do item 2 orally as well, then assign the page for independent work.

28

In, On, or Under?

Look at the picture and read the sentences next to it.

1. The book is *on* the desk.

2. The paper is *in* the desk.

3. The shoe is *under* the desk.

4. The ball is *behind* the desk.

5. The eraser is *next to* the book.

A Now look at the picture of Anne's room, and complete the sentences about it by writing *in*, *on*, *under*, *behind*, or *next to*.

1. The socks are _____ the shoes.

2. The jeans are _____ the floor.

3. Anne is _____ the table.

4. The tennis racket is _____ the chair.

5. The boots are _____ the sweater.

6. The blouse is _____ the chair.

7. The bathrobe is _____ the closet.

8. The records are _____ the bed.

Anne's Room

B In your notebook, write a paragraph about this picture using the sentences from Part A. Begin your paragraph with the following title and topic sentence.

Anne's Messy Room

Anne's room is messy.

SKILL OBJECTIVES: Using prepositions *in*, *on*, *under*, *behind*, *next to*; writing a paragraph. Write the highlighted prepositions on the board and check understanding of their meaning. Call attention to the top picture. Have students read the five sentences and demonstrate where the items are. *Part A:* Have students look at the picture of Anne's room and do the eight questions orally as a class before writing their answers. *Part B:* Discuss the sample paragraph on page 119 and tell students they are to write a paragaph about Anne's room using the sentences in Part A. Check for indentation, capitalization of the first word in a sentence, and a period at the end of each sentence.

Where Are My Things?

Write in the answers. The first one is done for you.

Language Objective
Describe locations of objects using prepositions.

1. Where are my shoes?

They're under the bed.

2. Where is my notebook?

3. Where is my green tie?

4. Where are my books?

5. Where are our jackets?

6. Where is my belt?

7. Where are my keys?

SKILL OBJECTIVE: Using prepositions *in, on, under, behind, in front of.* Review the highlighted prepositions, writing them on the board and having students demonstrate each one *(under, on, in, in front of, behind)*. Go through part or all of the page orally before assigning it for independent written work.

Fireworks

Read the story.

Language Objectives
Answer questions about a reading. Describe locations of people using prepositions.

Today is the Fourth of July. Kim's family and Tad's family are waiting to see the fireworks. Tad is looking in the picnic basket. Kim is hiding under a picnic table. His sister May is behind a tree. Kim's parents, Bob and Nancy, are sitting under the tree. They are talking to Tad's parents, Sam and Helen. They are all sitting on a picnic blanket. Next to the blanket is a basket. There is food in the basket. Yum!

After dark, the fireworks will start. They will go off high over people's heads. Tad can hardly wait. Kim isn't sure he will like the noise.

A **Answer the following questions. The first one is done for you.**

1. What day is it?   *It is the Fourth of July.*

2. Where is May hiding?   _____

3. Who is under a picnic table?   _____

4. Where are Kim's parents?   _____

5. Where is the picnic basket?   _____

6. What is everyone waiting to see?   _____

B **What is this story mostly about? Circle the best answer.**

a. Kim's parents

b. The basket of food

c. Kim's sister

d. Waiting to see the fireworks

C **Write the name of each person in the place where he or she is sitting. Be sure to include Kim, Tad, and their families.**

SKILL OBJECTIVES: Identifying main idea and details; following directions. Say, "Today is the Fourth of July. What do people do on the Fourth of July? Look at the picture. What are people doing?" Provide needed vocabulary as students suggest what is going on. Read the story aloud. Answer questions 2 and 3 as a class, then assign Parts A and B as independent written work. Discuss Part B when it is done. Remind students to reread the story as they independently complete Part C.

Maps

```
┌─────────────────────────────────────────────────────────────────────────┐
│  ┌──────┬──────┐   ┌──────┬──────┬──────┐        ┌────────────────┐       │
│  │Night-│Hotel │   │ Bank │ Drug │ Bus  │        │  Department    │       │
│  │ club │      │   │      │Store │Station│       │    Store       │       │
│  └──────┴──────┘   └──────┴──────┴──────┘        └────────────────┘       │
│                    WASHINGTON STREET                                       │
│  ┌──────────┐  S   ┌──────┬────────┐  P    ┌────────────────┐             │
│  │ Chinese  │  T   │Movie │ Police │  I    │    Church       │            │
│  │Restaurant│  A   │Theater│Station│  N    ├────────────────┤            │
│  ├──────────┤  T   ├──────┴────────┤  E    │  Post Office    │            │
│  │ Library  │  E   │ Parking Lot   │       └────────────────┘            │
│  ├──────────┤  Street              S       ┌────────────────┐            │
│  │ Hospital │      Park │Tennis│  T        │  Apartment     │            │
│  └──────────┘           │Courts│  R        │  Building      │            │
│                                  E                                        │
│                                  E                                        │
│                                  T                                        │
└─────────────────────────────────────────────────────────────────────────┘
```

A Answer *Yes* or *No* to the following statements. The first one is done for you.

1. The library is *between* the Chinese restaurant and the hospital.   _____Yes_____

2. The library is *on* State Street.   _____

3. The hotel is *next to* the hospital.   _____

4. The bank is *at the corner of* Washington Street and State Street.   _____

5. The hotel is *across from* the bank.   _____

B Use the words at the end of the line to answer these questions. The first one is done for you.

1. Where is the park?   _It's on State Street._____ (on)

2. Where is the drug store? _____ (between)

3. Where is the church? _____ at the corner of)

4. Where is the department store? _____ (across from)

5. Where is the post office? _____ (next to)

C Answer these questions. The first one is done for you.

1. Is the parking lot next to the movie theater?   _____Yes, it is._____

2. Is the police station between the church and the bank?   _____

3. Is the hospital across from the drug store?   _____

4. Is the bus station at the corner of Pine Street and Washington Street?   _____

5. Are the tennis courts next to the apartment building?   _____

Following Directions

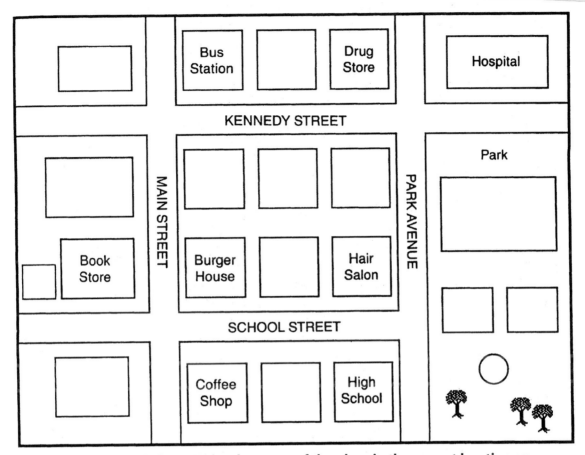

Read the sentences below. Write the name of the place in the correct location on the map.

1. The *hotel* is next to Burger House at the corner of Main Street and Kennedy Street.

2. The *bank* is between Burger House and the hair salon on School Street.

3. The *parking lot* is across from the bank, next to the high school.

4. The *gas station* is between the bus station and the drug store on Kennedy Street.

5. The *playground* is in the park. The *tennis courts* are in the park too.

6. The *music store* is across the street from the gas station, next to the hotel.

7. The *church* is at the corner of Main Street and School Street.

8. The *movie theater* is next to the music store at the corner of Park Avenue and Kennedy Street.

9. The *post office* is next to the bookstore at the corner of Main Street and Kennedy Street.

10. A *pay phone* is next to the bookstore.

11. The *library* is at the corner of Main Street and Kennedy Street.

12. A *drinking fountain* is near the tennis courts in the park.

SKILL OBJECTIVES: Reading a map; following directions. On the board write, *on, at the corner of, next to* and *across from*. Ask volunteers to use these words to describe orally the location of each named place on the map. Go over the instructions for the page and complete the first few items as a class, comparing and correcting each drawing. Note: To use this as a listening activity, write the names of the twelve places on the board and have students cover the sentences. Dictate the sentences to the class and have students write the name of each place in the correct location.

The Middle Atlantic States

Read the article.

Language Objectives
Answer questions about a reading. Use direction words to establish the location of states.

The Middle Atlantic States are the five states bordering on the mid-Atlantic Ocean. Those states are New Jersey, New York, Maryland, Delaware, and Pennsylvania.

These states are near each other. New Jersey is south of New York, east of Pennsylvania, and north of Delaware. Maryland is south of Pennsylvania, west of Delaware, and north of Virginia. The Atlantic Ocean is east of all of these states. New York, New Jersey, Delaware, and Maryland have coasts on the Atlantic Ocean.

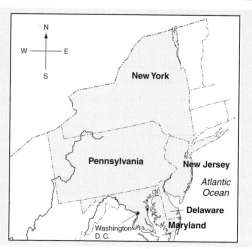

A **Answer the following questions. Fill in the circle.**

1. Where are the Middle Atlantic States? ⓐ ⓑ ⓒ
   a. to the west of Canada
   b. in the middle of the United States
   c. bordering the Atlantic Ocean

2. Which is *not* a Middle Atlantic state? ⓐ ⓑ ⓒ
   a. Virginia
   b. Delaware
   c. Pennsylvania

3. What state is next to New Jersey on the south? ⓐ ⓑ ⓒ
   a. New York
   b. Delaware
   c. Maryland

4. What state does not border on the Atlantic Ocean? ⓐ ⓑ ⓒ
   a. Maryland
   b. New York
   c. Pennsylvania

B **Look at the map and answer the following questions. Use the words *north*, *south*, *east*, and *west*.**

1. New York is _____ of Pennsylvania.
2. The Middle Atlantic States are _____ of the Atlantic Ocean.
3. Delaware is _____ of Maryland.
4. New York is _____ of New Jersey.
5. Pennsylvania is _____ of Washington, D.C.
6. New Jersey is _____ of New York.

C **In your notebook, write about the state you live in. Tell what is north, south, east, and west of it.**

SKILL OBJECTIVES: Reading a map; reading to find facts; writing a paragraph. Call attention to the map and pronounce the names of the states. Then discuss the directions: north, south, east, and west. If you have a map of the United States, you may wish to locate your own state and ask what states are north, south, east, and west of it. Read the article aloud. *Part A:* Do question 1 together to be sure students understand the format. *Part B:* Do item 1 orally and make sure students understand why east is the only correct answer. *Part C:* Students may need a U.S. map for this part. Also, refer them again to the model paragraph on page 119.

Unit 4 Using the Verb *To Be*

Describing People

Language Objective
Use the full form and the contraction form of the verb *to be* in sentences.

A   Fill in the missing words. The first one is done for you.

I am (I'm)	She is (She's)	We are (We're)	They are (They're)
He is (He's)	It is (It's)	You are (You're)	

1. Hello. I ____am____ Binh. I _____ from Vietnam.

2. This is my class. We _____ from different countries.

3. She _____ Anna. She _____ from Greece.

4. He _____ Amin. He _____ from Lebanon.

5. They _____ Luis and Rosa. They _____ from Mexico.

B   Write the correct form of the verb *to be* in the blanks. The first one is done for you.

1. The desk _____is_____ on the left.

2. The students _____ in the gym.

3. We _____ from London, England.

4. You _____ not Chinese.

5. The girls _____ tired.

6. It _____ 3:00.

7. His first name _____ Paul.

8. Mary and Henry _____ nervous about the test.

9. I _____ angry at the boys.

10. My friends _____ from Canada.

11. They _____ homesick for their country, Mexico.

12. September _____ before October.

13. Marjorie _____ wearing a T-shirt today.

14. We _____ all students.

SKILL OBJECTIVE: Reviewing present forms of *to be*. Ask students, "Where are you from? Where is (Paco, Binh) from? Where are (Tomas and Gina) from? Where are you and (Ali) from?" Use the responses to build a chart on the board with all the present forms of *to be* ("I am from …," "He is from …," etc.). Review the chart together. *Part A*: Do this as an oral exercise before assigning it as independent written work. *Part B*: Go over the first two sentences as an oral exercise before assigning the Part as independent work.

Anna Garcia

Language Objective
Describe a person.

A **Circle the best word. The first one is done for you.**

This is [Sam. / Alice. / Anna.]

[His / Her] last name is Garcia.

[He / She] is [chubby. / slim.]

[He / She] is [fifty-three. / thirteen.]

[He / She] is wearing [black / white] shoes,

a [black / white] shirt, and [gray / white] pants.

[His / Her] hair is [black / red / blonde] and [his / her] jacket is [black. / gray. / white.]

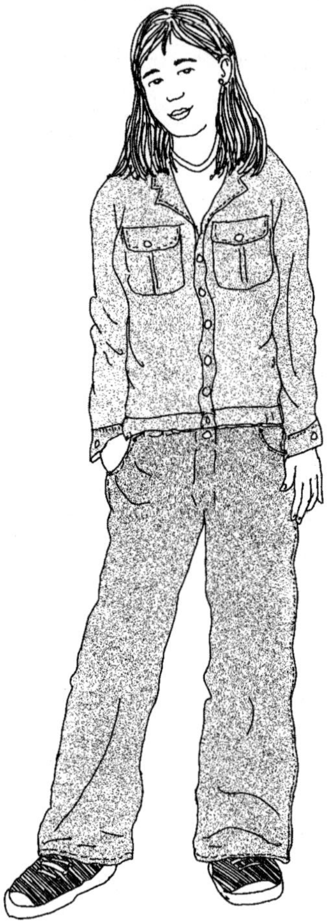

B **Describe your friend or your favorite star.**

____

____

____

____

____

SKILL OBJECTIVES: Reviewing pronouns and adjectives; writing a description. Briefly review the pronouns *he, she, his,* and *her* by asking students questions about their classmates: "What is (Anna's/Mario's) last name?" "Is (Laura/Carlos) tall or short?" "How old is your (sister/ brother)?" "What color is (Manuel's) hair?" Do Part A as an oral group exercise before assigning it as independent written work. Explain that students can use Part A as a model as they write their own descriptive paragraph in Part B. You may wish again to refer students to the model paragraph on page 119 for important parts of the paragraph format.

Describing People and Things

Write the sentences. Use the adjectives in the Data Bank.
The first two are done for you.

1.   Ted   Jan

84   14

a. _Ted is old._

b. _Jan is young._

2.   Linda   Gina

a. _____

b. _____

3.   Fluffy   Kitty

a. _____

b. _____

4.   Dress   Sweater

a. _____

b. _____

5. $200,000 $40

a. _____

b. _____

6.   They   He

a. _____

b. _____

DATA BANK

thin	~~young~~	single	cheap	tall	beautiful
expensive	short	~~old~~	married	fat	ugly

SKILL OBJECTIVE: Reviewing adjectives and present forms of to be. Encourage students to call out the opposites as you say the following words: *big, fat, expensive, tall, beautiful, old, good, different,* and *sad.* Ask volunteers to orally provide contrasting ("Opposite") sentences to go with each pair of sketches on the page. Students can refer to the Data Bank for appropriate adjectives. Assign the page for independent written work.

37

Information, Please

I am (I'm)	you are (you're)	he is (he's)	she is (she's)
it is (it's)	we are (we're)	you are (you're)	they are (they're)

Answer the questions. Use complete sentences. The first one is done for you.

1. What street is your school on? It's on _____ Street.

2. What day is it today? _____

3. Are you tired today? _____

4. What is your last name? _____

5. What is your favorite color? _____

6. Are your shoes black? _____

7. Are you twins? _____

8. Is English easy or difficult for you? _____

9. Where are your books? _____

10. Is your house big or small? _____

11. Are your friends young or old? _____

12. Is a new car cheap? _____

13. How old are you? _____

14. What time is it now? _____

15. What color are your eyes? _____

16. Are you tall or short? _____

17. Is your school beautiful or ugly? _____

18. What is your favorite school subject? _____

19. Who is your English teacher? _____

20. Is today a beautiful day? _____

21. Are cats large animals? _____

22. Where is your English class? _____

SKILL OBJECTIVE: Answering informational questions with present forms of *to be.* Review the present forms of the verb *to be* with all subject pronouns. Call attention to the abbreviations and point out that students can use either the full form or the abbreviated form. Do the first two questions orally with the class before assigning the page as independent written work.

Tiger Woods: Reading a Biography

Language Objectives
Answer questions about a reading. Write a short biography.

Read the article.

Tiger Woods is a famous golfer. He was born in 1975, in Cypress, California. Cypress is a town near Los Angeles. Tiger started playing golf when he was nine months of age! At age five, *Golf Digest*, a golf magazine, wrote an article about him. At age sixteen, he played in his first professional golf tournament. By age twenty-two, he was a superstar and named Player of the Year.

People everywhere love to watch Tiger play golf. He plays in many different countries and wins many professional championship games. Tiger lives in Florida now. His family is very proud of him.

A **Answer the following questions about Tiger Woods.** **The first one is done for you.**

1. Is Tiger Woods a baseball player? _____*No, he isn't.*_____

2. Is Tiger from California? _____

3. Why is Tiger famous? _____

4. Did Tiger like golf as a child? _____

5. How old is Tiger now? _____

6. How old was Tiger when he played his first golf tournament? _____

B **Read the sentences.** **Then circle the best answer.**

Tiger Woods was a good golf player as a child. Every year he became a better player. This means that people who play a sport _____.

a. have to play every day

b. can start playing at age two

c. are often more successful if they start at a young age

d. want to be famous

C **In your notebook, write about a famous person you like. Tell where he or she is from. Tell what he or she is famous for. Tell any other information you know. Your teacher or your librarian can help you find out about the person.**

SKILL OBJECTIVES: Reading a biography; making inferences; writing a paragraph. Read the article aloud and go over any vocabulary that may be new to the students. Ask them if they are fans of Tiger Woods or have ever seen him play golf on television. *Part A:* Do the first two questions orally. *Part B:* Students need to understand the words *golf* and *better player* before they can make an inference about athletes. *Part C:* "Famous persons" can include historical figures, other athletes, or people in the news.

Using Capital Letters

Capital letters are "large" letters. For example, the *B* in *Bob* is a capital letter. When you write, you need to use both capital and small letters. Here are some rules for using capital letters.

Rule 1:	Use a capital letter for the first word in every sentence.
	Example: **T**he boy is sitting on the chair.
Rule 2:	Use a capital letter for the first person singular (I).
	Example: My brother and **I** are going to Mexico.
Rule 3:	Use a capital letter for names of people, days of the week, months of the year, cities, and countries.
	Example: **T**om is going to **N**ew **Y**ork on **M**onday, the 5th of **D**ecember.
Rule 4:	Use a capital letter for the names of streets, schools, languages, and holidays.
	Example: The **E**nglish classes at the **A**dams **L**anguage **S**chool on **C**opley **S**treet start the day after **L**abor **D**ay.

A In your notebook, rewrite the following sentences, capitalizing words where necessary.

1. her sister is living in japan.

2. i want to be an architect when i finish school.

3. mr. johnson would like a carton of eggs at the store.

4. many schools in the united states begin classes in september.

5. november, december, and january are cold months in canada.

6. janet is talking with rosita perez, the principal.

7. mark and bill wear their green pants to work on saturdays.

8. gina is tall but i am short.

9. binh nguyen and his sister live on everett street.

10. we have a test in english this friday.

11. the flag of colombia is red, blue, and yellow.

12. columbus day is always on monday and always in october.

13. the capital of ohio is columbus and the capital of south carolina is columbia.

14. people in france celebrate bastille day every year in july.

15. boston university is on commonwealth avenue in boston, but boston college is on commonwealth avenue in newton.

SKILL OBJECTIVE: Following rules for capitalization. On the board, explain the difference between capital and lowercase letters. Go over the rule box, asking volunteers to read the four rules and asking other students to come up and write different examples of each rule. After ample practice, explain the directions, do the first sentence together, and assign the remaining sentences as independent written work.

Letters to a Friend

Dear Rosanna,

   This is a picture of my boyfriend, Manuel. He's tall and slim and he's very handsome! His hair is black, and in this picture he's wearing a sweater and jeans.

Your friend,
Lisa

Dear Ben,

   This is my new girlfriend. Her first name is Julia and her last name is Garcia. She is a Mexican American. Her mother is from Texas, and her father is from Acapulco. She's short. She's 14 and very friendly and pretty.

Your friend,
Carlos

Write a letter to a friend. Draw a picture of someone you know—a real person or a star.

Dear _____

_____

_____

_____

_____

_____

_____

_____

41

What's His Name?

Read the story.

Language Objectives
Answer questions about a reading. Write a short essay about names and nicknames.

> My name is Manuel Rodriguez. At school, I am Manuel. At home, my name is Manolo. With my friends, I am Papo. With my basketball coach, I am Rodriguez. At work, I am Manny. I am a boy with many names!

A **What is his name with:**

1. his math teacher? _____

2. his mother? _____

3. his sister? _____

4. his friend Pablo? _____

5. his coach? _____

6. his principal? _____

7. his boss? _____

8. his father? _____

B **What is this story mostly about? Circle the best answer.**

a. Manuel and his family.

b. Manuel and his teachers.

c. Manuel and his names.

d. Manuel and his friends.

C **Are you a person with more than one name, too? Write a paragraph like Manuel's.**

Hi! My name is _____

_____

_____

_____

_____

SKILL OBJECTIVES: Identifying main idea and details; writing a paragraph. Ask several students to give their full names and nicknames ("What does your family call you? What do your friends call you?" etc.) List the full names and nicknames on the board. Read the story aloud, or have students read it silently. *Part A:* Have students answer orally, then assign for writing. *Part B:* After students choose the main idea have them discuss why each choice is correct or incorrect. *Part C:* Students should model their paragraphs after the story at the top. (For paragraph format, they may also refer to the model paragraph on page 119.)

Dear Dot

Dear Dot,
 I am a girl with long, dark hair and dark eyes, and so is my sister. My favorite color is blue, and so is my sister's. We are both tennis players. We are twins! We are happy being twins, but here is our problem; boys don't know who is who, so they don't ask us out. They feel nervous and silly because they can't tell us apart. I'm staying home too many Friday nights, and so is my sister. What can we do?

Lonely Twin

1. How are the sisters alike? _____

_____

_____

2. What is their problem? _____

_____

3. Why do the boys feel nervous and silly? _____

_____

4. What is your advice for Lonely Twin? Circle your answer.

   a. Be different from your sister.

   b. Call up boys and ask them for dates.

   c. Wear a name tag.

   d. Go out alone on Friday nights.

5. Now read Dot's answer. See if your answer is the same. If your answer is different, tell why you disagree. Dot's advice is below.

Dear Lonely Twin,
 You and your sister are too much alike. Change your hair style. Wear different colors. Play different sports. If that doesn't work, wear name tags!
Dot

SKILL OBJECTIVES: Reading comprehension; making judgments. Read the letter aloud as students follow along. Explain any unfamiliar words. Ask students to reread the letter silently, then answer questions 1–4. Correct the first three answers, then let students compare their choice of advice. Read Dot's answer together. Let students say why they agree or disagree with Dot's reply and perhaps offer some other suggestions.

Unit **5** Food

Food and Drink

Language Objectives
Name common foods.
Answer questions about food.

A Learn the words for the foods below. Find the words in the Data Bank, then write each word on the line.

1. _____

2. _____

3. _____

4. _____

5. _____

6. _____

7. _____

8. _____

9. _____

10. _____

11. _____

12. _____

13. _____

14. _____

15. _____

B Answer the following questions about the foods above. Circle the correct answer. The first one is done for you.

1. What food is red, yellow, or green?

   a. fish   **b.** carrots   **c.** apples

2. What food is good for a sandwich?

   a. peanuts   **b.** cheese   **c.** ice cream

3. What food is from a chicken?

   a. beans   **b.** eggs   **c.** cheese

4. What food is long and orange?

   a. chicken   **b.** pears   **c.** carrots

5. What food is yellow and sweet?

   a. bananas   **b.** meat   **c.** grapes

DATA BANK

apples	carrots	eggs	ice cream	mushrooms
bananas	cheese	fish	lettuce	nuts
beans	chicken	grapes	meat	pears

SKILL OBJECTIVES: Learning food vocabulary; answering multiple-choice questions. *Part A:* Introduce or review the vocabulary. Point out the plural forms used for items 1, 2, 4, 6, 7, 8, 11, 12, and call attention to the Data Bank at the bottom of the page where all fifteen answers will be found. *Part B:* Point out that these items are in another multiple-choice format. Show how the first answer has been marked by circling "c. apples." Discuss why this answer is correct and why the others are not. Then assign the page for independent written work.

Doing Things

You can use *am, is,* or *are* plus a word with *-ing* to tell what someone is doing. Look at these sentences.

I am eating a steak.	We are eating eggs.	You are eating an apple.
She is drinking tea.	He is cooking fish.	They are buying ice cream.

A Look at the pictures below. Write a sentence on the line to tell what the people or animals are doing. Use Data Bank A to help you. The first one is done for you.

1. _It is drinking._   2. _____   3. _____

4. _____   5. _____   6. _____

DATA BANK A

eating	drinking	cooking	buying

B What are these people doing? Write a sentence on the line. Use Data Bank B.

1. _____   2. _____

 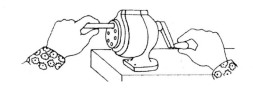

3. _____   4. _____

DATA BANK B

opening their books	sharpening her pencil
walking in the hall	paying attention to the teacher

SKILL OBJECTIVES: Recognizing subject pronouns; present progressive tense. *Part A:* Call attention to picture 1 and ask, "What is the cat doing?" Have a volunteer read the sentence under the picture. Ask similar questions for pictures 2 through 6. Students are to use the correct pronoun and one of the words in Data Bank A for their answers. After all questions have been done orally, have students write their answers. *Part B:* Use a similar procedure. Students will use one of the phrases in Data Bank B for each item.

Salads for Everyone!

Language Objectives
Agree or disagree about food prices. Practice a dialogue about food and its price.

Read the menu of *Salads for Everyone*. Then do the exercises.

Salads for Everyone — MENU

Green salad	$4.00	Chicken salad sandwich	$3.25
Mushroom salad	$5.50	Ham and tomato sandwich	$3.75
Egg salad	$6.00	Turkey and Swiss cheese	
Bean salad	$6.50	on pita bread	$3.50
		Coffee	$1.75
Tomato soup	$3.75	Tea	$1.75
Onion soup	$4.25	Iced green tea	$2.50
		Carrot juice	$1.75
Regular milk	$1.50	Apple juice	$2.00
Health shakes (soy, half-and-		Banana smoothie	$2.50
half, skim milk)			
Regular	$2.50		
Large	$3.00		

A **Add up these bills. Are they correct?**   **Yes or No?**

1. A green salad and tea is $6.00.   _____

2. An egg salad and iced green tea is $8.50.   _____

3. A bean salad, onion soup, and carrot juice is $11.00.   _____

4. A ham and tomato sandwich and a regular health shake is $6.25.   _____

5. A chicken salad sandwich and tomato soup is $8.00.   _____

6. A green salad, regular milk, and apple juice is $7.50.   _____

B **You are at Salads for Everyone. Practice this conversation with a classmate.**

A: Welcome to *Salads for Everyone*. What would you like today?

B: I would like a _____, please.

A: Would you like something to drink as well?

B: Oh, sure. Could I have _____?

A: Of course. Your total is $ _____.

B: Thanks so much!

A: Our pleasure. Have a great day!

C **In your notebook, write about a kind of food you like. Say why you like this food.**

SKILL OBJECTIVES: Practicing money skills; using a chart. *Part A:* Discuss the menu with the class. Then ask a student to place his or her order. Say, "Can I help you?" If necessary, add, "Anything to drink?" after the student has ordered. Write the student's order on the board. Have the class find the price of each item, then calculate the total bill. Repeat several times, then lassign Part A for independent work. *Part B:* Allow time for students to role play; circulate and provide help, if necessary. *Part C:* Discuss different kinds of food and which ones students prefer. Then have them write about their favorite food.

More Food

1. sausage
2. lobster
3. black beans
4. strawberries
5. shrimps
6. clams
7. hamburger
8. spare ribs
9. pork chops
10. melon
11. tomatoes
12. onions
13. cherries
14. rice
15. peppers
16. tuna
17. roast beef
18. corn
19. cucumbers
20. potatoes

Look at the pictures of the foods above. Then look at the names of the four food groups below. Decide which group each food belongs in and write its name under the heading for that group. The first one is done for you.

Meat	Seafood	Vegetables	Fruits
sausage			

SKILL OBJECTIVES: Building vocabulary; classifying. Let volunteers name familiar food pictures. Then teach the new vocabulary items. Play a cumulative list game for vocabulary reinforcement. Student A will say, "I am eating (pork chops) for dinner." The next student will repeat that and add a food of his/her own: "I am eating pork chops and (sausage) for dinner." Students do not have to limit themselves to the foods on this page. Call attention to the chart at the bottom of the page. Work as a group to classify the first few foods. Then let students complete the chart independently.

In the Cafeteria

It's lunch time at Roosevelt High School. Binh, Rosa, and Tom are waiting in line.

TOM: What's for lunch today?
ROSA: I think it's pizza.
BINH: I hope so. I love pizza.
TOM: Not me. I don't like pizza. I like tacos.
ROSA: I'm not very hungry. I only want a salad.

Now Binh, Rosa, and Tom are at the front of the line. Mrs. May is serving lunch.

BINH: What's for lunch, Mrs. May?
MRS. MAY: Fried chicken.
ROSA: I'll have that.
TOM: Me too.
BINH: The same for me.

Mrs. May smiles and gives the students their lunch.

A **Answer the questions about the dialogue. Fill in the circles.**

1. Where do the students go to school?　　　　ⓐ　ⓑ　ⓒ
   a. in the cafeteria
   b. for pizza
   c. at Roosevelt High School

2. What food does Binh love?　　　　ⓐ　ⓑ　ⓒ
   a. pizza
   b. tacos
   c. salad

3. What does Tom say about pizza?　　　　ⓐ　ⓑ　ⓒ
   a. He's eating it for lunch.
   b. He isn't hungry for pizza.
   c. He doesn't like it.

4. Who is Mrs. May?　　　　ⓐ　ⓑ　ⓒ
   a. a teacher at the school
   b. Tom's mother
   c. a cafeteria worker

5. Which of the following is true about the students in the dialogue?　　　　ⓐ　ⓑ　ⓒ
   a. They like pizza.
   b. They want salads.
   c. They like fried chicken.

B **In your notebook, make a chart with two columns like the one you see here. Complete the chart with your own food likes and dislikes.**

Food I Like	Food I Don't Like

SKILL OBJECTIVE: **Using information to make inferences.** *Part A:* Do question 1 orally with the class to be sure students remember how to mark their answers. *Part B:* Students can use the vocabulary from pages 44, 46, and 47 in making their lists.

Buying Food

A Write the words. The first one is done for you.

1. a can of tuna

2. _____

3. _____

4. _____

5. _____

6. _____

7. _____

8. _____

9. _____

10. _____

11. _____

12. _____

DATA BANK		
a carton of eggs	a head of lettuce	a can of tuna
a box of cereal	a bag of onions	a bottle of oil
a quart of juice	a gallon of milk	a jar of peanut butter
a pound of hamburger	a bunch of carrots	a loaf of bread

B Circle the word that doesn't belong. The first one is done for you.

1. hamburger	(lettuce)	sausage	roast beef
2. large	small	medium	first
3. coffee	fish	milk	lemonade
4. picture	drug store	school	restaurant
5. near	across	is	in
6. bed	table	shoe	chair
7. eggs	box	can	jar
8. second	three o'clock	ten thirty	quarter of one
9. tall	old	fat	man
10. bacon	eggs	toast	ice cream

SKILL OBJECTIVES: Building vocabulary; reviewing food vocabulary; classifying. *Part A:* If possible, bring in a variety of groceries to teach vocabulary. Include boxes, bags, cans, quart containers, etc. Have students locate the weight or capacity on the container. Have them list other goods that are packaged in cans, boxes, etc. Teach or review the vocabulary on the page, go over the instructions for Part A and assign it for independent written work. *Part B:* This is a classifying activity. Ask for volunteers to tell why lettuce is circled in the first item. Do a few more examples orally, then assign for independent work.

A or An?

Use *an* before a vowel (a, e, i, o, u) or a vowel sound.

| an apple | an egg | an hour | an honest man |

Use *a* before a consonant (b, c, d, f, g, h, j, k, l, m, n, p, q, r, s, t, v, w, x, y, z) or a consonant-sounding vowel.

| a banana | a used car | a teacher | a yellow box |

Fill in with *a* or *an*. Then practice reading the sentences aloud with a classmate.

1. He is reading ___*an*___ English book.

2. Lisa is _____ pretty girl.

3. Tom is eating _____ apple.

4. Mrs. Thompson is _____ old woman.

5. Maria is buying _____ banana and _____ pear.

6. James is studying at _____ university in New York.

7. Luis is eating _____ orange.

8. Mrs. Lee is wearing _____ red dress.

9. My father is _____ honest man.

10. She is eating _____ egg for breakfast.

11. Paul is looking at _____ new car.

12. David is _____ thin boy.

13. The baby is eating _____ ice cream cone.

14. The boy is buying _____ umbrella.

15. Sandra is wearing _____ orange coat.

16. Michael is wearing _____ blue shirt.

17. Sally is _____ eight-year-old girl.

18. Mr. Jones is _____ happy man.

19. The boy is eating _____ carrot.

20. Jack is sitting on _____ chair.

SKILL OBJECTIVE: Using articles *a* and *an*. Go over the rules at the top of the page with the class. Point out that *an* is used in words beginning with a silent *h: an hour, an honest man*. The article *a* is used before words beginning with a long *u: a used car*. Practice the examples and other words orally before assigning the page for independent and pair work.

Questions with *Like*

Many students are confused by questions with the word *like*. Look at the following box.

Language Objectives
Answer questions about a reading. Distinguish between different meanings of the word <u>like</u>.

Like question	Explanation	Possible answer
"What would you like?"	This means the same as "What do you want?"	"I would like a pizza."
"What sports do you like?"	This means the same as "What sports are your favorites?"	"I like hockey and soccer."
"What do you look like?"	This means the same as "How do you describe yourself?"	"I'm tall with black hair and blue eyes." (Notice that "look like" is not part of the answer.)

A **Now read the following story and answer the questions.**

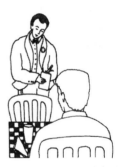

John Perry is in a restaurant. He is hungry and he would like to eat a big dinner. He calls the waiter. He says, "I'd like a steak, french fries, and a large salad." John Perry is an athlete. He is 6 feet tall and weighs 170 pounds. He has blond hair and brown eyes. John is so hungry because he played sports all day. In the morning he played basketball. In the afternoon he played soccer. Those are his favorite sports.

1. What does John Perry look like? —————————————

————————————————————————————————

2. What would John like to eat? —————————————

————————————————————————————————

3. What sports does John like to play? ———————————

————————————————————————————————

B **What about you? Answer the following questions in your notebook.**

1. What do you look like?

2. What sports do you like?

3. What would you like to eat for dinner tonight?

Ask five other people these three questions. Write down their answers in your notebook.

SKILL OBJECTIVE: Differentiating among uses of *like*. Before assigning the page, prepare several additional examples of each *like* meaning to be sure students understand the difference. *Part A:* Read the paragraph orally together and go over any new vocabulary. Then do question 1 orally with the class. *Part B:* Discuss the three questions. Then have students write answers about themselves. Have them interview five others, using the same questions and writing these persons' answers. As an extension, you may wish to have the class chart the results of their interviews.

Dear Dot

Dear Dot,

My mother is on a diet. My sister is on a diet. My grandmother is on a diet. I am NOT on a diet, and there is nothing good to eat in my house. I like steak and pork chops, potatoes, and rice. I want an ice cream or a pizza NOW! My mother is eating only salad and fish. My sister is eating only carrots, cucumbers, and tomatoes. My grandmother is eating only chicken and lettuce. I am STARVING! What can I do?

A Hungry Boy

1. Who is on a diet? _____

2. What does the boy like? _____

3. What is his mother eating? _____

4. What is his sister eating? _____

5. What is his grandmother eating? _____

6. What is your advice for Hungry Boy? Circle your answer.

    a. Go on a diet, too.   **c.** Eat only candy; don't eat at home.

    b. Go to a restaurant to eat every night.   **d.** Eat diet meals at home and other food outside.

7. Now read Dot's answer. See if your answer is the same. If your answer is different, tell why you disagree. Dot's advice is below.

Dear Hungry Boy,
Eat at a friend's house. Eat the food you like at lunch. Learn to like salad and fish and chicken. Buy some snacks and eat them before you go home. But be careful! You don't want to be on a diet, too.

Dot

SKILL OBJECTIVES: Reading comprehension; making judgments. Have students recall the previous "Dear Dot" page (page 43). Read Hungry Boy's letter aloud as students follow along. Explain any unfamiliar words. Ask students to reread the letter silently, then answer questions 1–6. Correct the first five answers, then let students compare their choice of advice. Read Dot's answer together. Let students tell why they agree or disagree with Dot's reply and perhaps offer some other solutions.

The Peterson Family

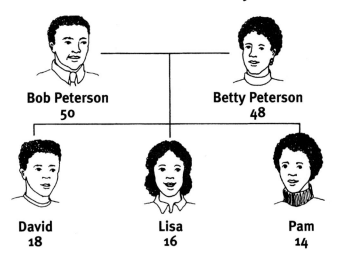

Bob and Betty Peterson are married. Betty is Bob's wife. Bob is Betty's husband. Betty and Bob are parents of three children. David is 18 years old. David is Bob and Betty's son. Lisa and Pam are Bob and Betty's daughters. David is Lisa and Pam's brother. Lisa and Pam are David's sisters. Bob is their father. Betty is their mother.

A **Answer these questions. The first one is done for you.**

1. Who is the husband?   Bob
2. Who is the wife?   _____
3. Who are the parents?   _____
4. Who is the son?   _____
5. Who are the daughters?   _____
6. Who are the children?   _____
7. Who are David's sisters?   _____
8. Who is Pam and Lisa's brother?   _____

B **Answer *Yes* or *No* to the following statements.**

___No___ 1. Bob is married to Pam.

_____ 2. Bob and Betty are the parents of three children.

_____ 3. Pam and Lisa are brothers.

_____ 4. David is Bob and Betty's daughter.

_____ 5. David is the father.

_____ 6. Bob Peterson is fifty years old.

_____ 7. David, Lisa, and Betty are the children.

_____ 8. Betty and Pam are sisters.

DATA BANK					
family	parents	father	husband	daughter	children
mother	married	son	sister	wife	brother

SKILL OBJECTIVES: Building vocabulary; answering questions. Teach or review the vocabulary on the page. Read the story about the Peterson family aloud. *Part A:* Work through the first three questions orally with the class. Then assign Part A as independent written work. *Part B:* Remind students to write *Yes* or *No* for each statement in Part B.

Amy's Family

Language Objectives
Explain family relationships.
Answer questions in the negative.

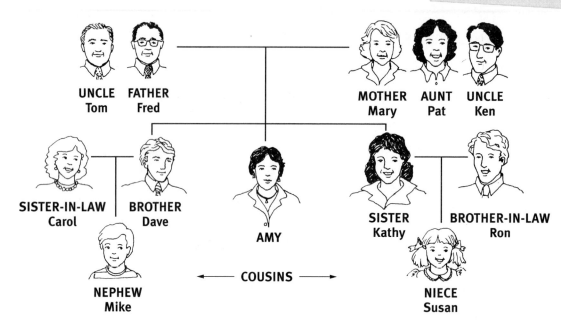

UNCLE Tom FATHER Fred MOTHER Mary AUNT Pat UNCLE Ken

SISTER-IN-LAW Carol BROTHER Dave AMY SISTER Kathy BROTHER-IN-LAW Ron

NEPHEW Mike ← COUSINS → NIECE Susan

A **Explain each person's relationship to Amy. The first one is done for you.**

1. Kathy _____ *She's Amy's sister.* _____

2. Mike _____

3. Fred _____

4. Ron _____

5. Pat _____

6. Susan _____

7. Ken _____

8. Tom _____

B **Complete the *No* answers with an explanation.**

1. Is Carol Amy's sister? _____ *No, she's Amy's sister-in-law.* _____

2. Is Mary Amy's aunt? _____ *No,* _____

3. Is Pat Mary's cousin? _____ *No,* _____

4. Is Susan Carol's daughter? _____ *No,* _____

5. Is Tom Fred's father? _____ *No,* _____

6. Is Mike Susan's brother? _____ *No,* _____

7. Is Ron Susan's uncle? _____ *No,* _____

8. Is Tom Pat's uncle? _____ *No,* _____

SKILL OBJECTIVES: Building vocabulary; understanding a "family tree" chart. Examine the family chart with the students. Ask questions about each person. Review such familiar terms as *brother* and introduce new terms such as *sister-in-law*. Ask, "Who is Amy's sister-in-law? To whom is she married?" *Part A:* Work through the first four items orally before assigning Part A for independent written work. *Part B:* Make sure students understand that the answer to all the questions is "No," and that they must tell what the relationship actually is. Do the first four items orally with the class, then assign Part B for independent written work.

54

Mr., Mrs., Miss, and Ms.

**Many students are confused by the titles *Mr., Mrs., Miss,* and *Ms.*
Read the explanation in the box.**

> **Mr.** (pronounced mis'ter) always refers to a man, married or single (not married).
>
> **Mrs.** (pronounced miss'is) refers to a married woman (or one who was married).
>
> **Miss** refers to a single woman (a woman who is not married and was never married).
>
> **Ms.** (pronounced mizz) refers to any woman, married or single.

A **Look at the following names. Circle *male* if the person is a male (a man) or *female* if the person is a female (a woman). Circle *S* if the person is single or *M* if the person is married. Circle *?* if it is not possible to tell if the person is single or married.**

1. Mr. Jamie Sullivan	male / female	S	M	?
2. Mrs. John Jones	male / female	S	M	?
3. Miss Pat Wu	male / female	S	M	?
4. Mr. Tracey Rogers	male / female	S	M	?
5. Ms. M. L. West	male / female	S	M	?
6. Mrs. P. X. Kennedy	male / female	S	M	?
7. Ms. Jordan Karr	male / female	S	M	?
8. Miss Dana Dorland	male / female	S	M	?

B **Write the names of some males and females you know. Use name titles, for example,
Mr. Liem Nguyen, Miss Melida Muñoz.**

Males	**Females**
_____	_____
_____	_____
_____	_____
_____	_____

C **Some women prefer to be called *Miss* or *Mrs.* Some prefer to be called *Ms.* Talk about this with some of your classmates. Then write in your notebook why you think a woman might choose to be called *Ms.* instead of *Miss* or *Mrs.***

SKILL OBJECTIVE: Learning pronouncing; distinguishing among different name titles. Go over the information in the box with the students, and answer questions. *Part A:* Work through the first two examples with the class. Be sure students understand the terms *male* and *female.* As students volunteer answers for the first column (male/female), ask, "How do you know?" Do the same with the second column (S, M, ?). *Part B:* You may wish to have students use the names of classmates or family members. Check to be sure they understand the directions. *Part C:* Assign to students who need challenge. You may wish to use it only as a discussion question.

Where Are They?

A **Answer the questions. The first one is done for you.**

1. Are you in the bedroom?

No, I'm not.
I'm in the kitchen.

2. Is the cat in the yard?

_____

_____

3. Is Cathy on her bike?

_____

_____

4. Is Vassily under the car?

_____

_____

B **Write the questions.**

1. _____

_____

No, they aren't.

They're in the bathtub.

2. _____

_____

No, we aren't.

We're in front of the fireplace.

3. _____

_____

No, he isn't.

He's behind the tree.

4. _____

_____

No, they aren't.

They're under the bed.

SKILL OBJECTIVES: Forming contractions; reviewing prepositions. Set classroom objects on a desk. Example: a stack of different colored books, an eraser behind the books, a box with pencils in front of the books. Ask questions beginning "Is/Are . . .?" ("Are the books under the desk?") Students should answer with a negative contraction, then give the correct information using a pronoun contraction. ("No, they aren't. They're on the desk.") Encourage students to ask each other questions. Work orally, then assign the page for independent written work.

Bill's Apartment Building

Language Objectives
State locations. Group related words in a category.

A Write the answers. Use *on* or *in*.

1. Where is the lobby?

   It's on the first floor.

2. Where is the laundry room?

   _____

3. Where is Bill's apartment?

   _____

4. Where is the TV antenna?

   _____

5. Where is the balcony?

   _____

6. Where is the manager's office?

   _____

7. Where is Mrs. Doe's apartment?

   _____

8. Where is the store room?

   _____

B Bill's apartment has four rooms. What is in each room? Use the Data Bank to fill in the chart. You may write each word more than once.

Living room	Kitchen	Bedroom	Bathroom

DATA BANK
armchair   chair   mirror   shower   stove   toilet
bathtub   dresser   refrigerator   sink   table   TV
bed   lamp   rug   sofa

SKILL OBJECTIVES: Building vocabulary; classifying. *Part A:* Discuss the apartment building. Establish that there are three floors and a basement. Ask, "What's on the first floor? Where is the laundry room?" etc. Listen for correct use of *in* and *on*. Ask students, "Do you live in an apartment building? What floor do you live on? What rooms do you have in your apartment?" Go over the questions orally before assigning them as independent written work. *Part B:* Teach/review the vocabulary in the Data Bank. Categorize the first few items as a group, then assign as independent written work.

What Are They Doing?

		Present Progressive		
I am working.	He / She / It	is working.	You / We / They	are working.

Write a sentence to go with each picture. Use the model above as a guide. The first one is done for you.

1. _He is writing._

2. _____

3. _____

4. _____

5. _____

6. _____

7. _____

8. _____

9. _____

10. _____

11. _____

12. _____

DATA BANK

watching	reading	shopping	driving	running	eating
dancing	riding	~~writing~~	sleeping	playing	washing

SKILL OBJECTIVE: Practicing the present progressive tense. Teach/review the vocabulary in the Data Bank. Have each verb pronounced. If there is confusion about the meaning of any verb, ask volunteers to act that verb out. Then go through the page orally. Other volunteers can suggest sentences for each picture, using the sample sentence under the first picture as a model. Monitor answers for correct subject pronouns. After sufficient oral practice, assign the page as independent written work.

Spell-*ing*

A There are a few rules to follow when you add -*ing* to a word.

Rule 1:	For most words, add -*ing* with no changes.
	Example: walk ➔ walking
Rule 2:	For words that end in silent (not pronounced) -*e*, drop the -*e* and add -*ing*.
	Example: dance ➔ dancing
Rule 3:	For one-syllable words that end in consonant–vowel–consonant (except *x*, *w*, and *l*), double the last letter and add -*ing*.
	Example: sit ➔ sitting

B Add -*ing* to each of the words below. All of the words are from pages in this book. They are words you know already. Follow the rules.

Rule 1: Add -*ing* with no change.

1. talk _____
2. open _____
3. wear _____
4. eat _____
5. wait _____

6. shout _____
7. call _____
8. buy _____
9. listen _____
10. study _____

Rule 2: Drop the final -*e* and add -*ing*.

11. come _____
12. erase _____
13. give _____
14. take _____
15. drive _____

16. raise _____
17. live _____
18. write _____
19. ride _____
20. type _____

Rule 3: Double the final consonant and add -*ing*.

21. run _____
22. shop _____
23. stop _____

24. get _____
25. spot _____
26. hit _____

C In your notebook, write a sentence for each -*ing* word.

Example: *He is talking to the teacher.*

SKILL OBJECTIVE: Learning spelling rules for adding -*ing*. *Part A:* Read over the box with the students. Add several more examples for each rule. (Try to avoid using the verbs in Part B.) Make sure that students understand the concept of "silent -e," and that they understand what a one-syllable consonant-vowel-consonant verb is. *Part B:* Do one or two examples for each rule with the class, then assign as independent written work. *Part C:* After students have written their sentences, ask each one to read his/her favorite sentence to the class.

The Kent Family at Home

Here are some questions about the Kent family. There are three answers after each question. Read all three answers. Decide which is the best answer and fill in the correct circle. The first one is done for you.

1. Where is Mr. Kent? (a) ● (c)

  a. He's in the garage.

  b. He's in the kitchen.

  c. He's in the yard.

5. What is Mrs. Kent doing? (a) (b) (c)

  a. She's cooking.

  b. She's reading a book.

  c. She's eating dinner.

2. What is he doing? (a) (b) (c)

  a. He's cooking dinner.

  b. He's watching TV.

  c. He's playing tennis.

6. Where are the boys? (a) (b) (c)

  a. They are in the kitchen.

  b. They are in the living room.

  c. They are in the yard.

3. Are the pets in the house? (a) (b) (c)

  a. The dog is in the house.

  b. No, they aren't.

  c. They are sleeping.

7. Where are the girls? (a) (b) (c)

  a. They are in the bedroom.

  b. They are in the kitchen.

  c. They are in the yard.

4. Where is Mrs. Kent? (a) (b) (c)

  a. She's in the yard.

  b. She's in the kitchen.

  c. She's in the living room.

8. What are they doing? (a) (b) (c)

  a. They are washing the car.

  b. They are doing homework.

  c. They are listening to music.

SKILL OBJECTIVES: Present progressive; reviewing vocabulary; answering multiple-choice questions. Discuss the picture with the class. Ask questions such as "How many daughters/sons do Mr. and Mrs. Kent have? Where are they? What are they doing?" After sufficient oral practice, go over question 1 to be sure students understand the directions before assigning the page as independent written work.

Two Families

Each year, many young people come to the United States from other countries. You are going to read about two of these young people and their families.

Language Objectives
Tell if a statement is true or false. Complete sentences by supplying a missing word.

Pablo's Family

Hi! My name is Pablo. I am fourteen years old. I am from Mexico City, Mexico. I am a ninth grade student at Grant High School. School is great. I like social studies and science the best.

I live with my family in Los Angeles. My father owns a small grocery store.

My mother works in a doctor's office. I have one brother and one sister. My brother, José, is five. My sister, Marta, is seven. I like my family a lot.

A Now read each sentence. Write *T* if the sentence is true. Write *F* if it is false. Write *?* if the story doesn't tell you the answer. The first two are done for you.

1. This boy's name is Pablo. _____T_____
2. His mother is forty years old. _____?_____
3. Pablo is from Russia. _____
4. Pablo owns a grocery store. _____
5. Marta likes movies. _____
6. Pablo's father is on vacation. _____
7. Pablo's brother is older than he is. _____
8. Pablo is five feet tall. _____
9. He lives in Mexico City. _____
10. Pablo likes science and social studies. _____

B Write one word in each space to complete the story of Shen's family.

Shen's Family

Hi! My name is Shen Wi. I _____ from Taipei. Taipei _____ a city in the country of Taiwan. I _____ twelve years old. I live _____ Austin, Texas, with my family.

My father _____ a lawyer. His office is downtown. My mother is a florist. People from all over the city order flowers from her shop. My older brother, Bobby, _____ seventeen years old. He _____ going to go to college next year. My younger sister, Sally, _____ to school at Lee Elementary. She _____ going to be ten in April. My family _____ terrific!

C Write a paragraph about your own family in your notebook.

SKILL OBJECTIVES: Answering true/false questions; completing a cloze exercise; writing a paragraph. *Part A:* Read the story of Pablo aloud as the students follow along. Ask true/false questions about the story. Then ask one or two questions that the students can't possibly answer from the story, so they understand the *?* component. The first two statements are already marked; go through them to be sure students understand why these answers are correct. Do several other items orally before assigning Part A for independent work. *Part B:* Be sure students understand what to do. You may wish to do the whole exercise orally before having students do it in writing.

Writing Questions

Language Objective
Ask questions using <u>to be</u> and present progressive (<u>-ing</u>) forms.

Read this paragraph about Robert's neighborhood.

It's a sunny Saturday, and everyone in Robert's neighborhood is outside today. Robert is riding his new bicycle. His next-door neighbor, David, is washing his car in the driveway. David's father is mowing the lawn. His other neighbors, Bill and Teddy, are playing ball in their yard. Their parents are playing ball, too. It's a nice day to be outside!

A **Write *yes/no* questions about the paragraph. Use the verb *to be*. See the model below. The first one is done for you.**

Am I busy?	Is { he / she / it } busy?	Are { you / we / they } busy?

1. ___Is it Saturday?___   Yes, it is.

2. _____ No, everyone is outside.

3. _____ No, David isn't his brother.

4. _____ Yes, he's in the driveway.

5. _____ Yes, he is. (David's father is at home.)

6. _____ No, they are in the yard.

7. _____ Yes, it is.

8. _____ No, I am not.

B **Write *yes/no* questions using the present progressive (*-ing*) form. See the model.**

Am I working?	Is { he / she / it } working?	Are { you / we / they } working?

1. _____? No, he's riding his bicycle.

2. _____? Yes, he is. (He's washing his car.)

3. _____? No, he's mowing the lawn.

4. _____? Yes, they are. (They're playing ball.)

5. _____? Yes, they are playing with them.

SKILL OBJECTIVES: Asking questions using *to be*; present progressive. Read the story about Robert's neighborhood aloud with the class. *Part A*: Discuss the models in the box. Then go through the eight items orally before having students write the questions. *Part B*: Discuss the models in the box. Work through the items orally before having students write the questions.

Dear Dot

Dear Dot,
My problem is, my father is never home. He is a sales representative, and he is always going to the airport or the train station or the bus station. He is working in Los Angeles this week. Next week he is going to Chicago. When my father IS at home, he is tired, or he is working in his office. What can I do?

Lonely Son

1. What's the boy's problem? _____

_____

2. What's his father's occupation? _____

_____

3. What's his father doing this week? _____

_____

4. Where is his father going next week? _____

_____

5. What is your advice for Lonely Son?

   a. Don't bother your father.

   c. Talk with your father about your feelings.

   b. Become a sales representative, too.

   d. Surprise your father and meet him in Chicago.

6. Now read Dot's answer. See if your answer is the same. If your answer is different, tell why you disagree. Dot's advice is below.

> Dear Lonely Son,
> Many young people write to me with the same problem. Fathers and mothers are working hard and spending less time with their children. Talk to your father; tell him you want to spend more time with him. Maybe you can go with him on a short trip. Tell him you want to do things with him on the weekends. Remember, he's working hard to take care of you.
>
> Dot

SKILL OBJECTIVES: Reading comprehension; making judgments. Read the letter aloud as students follow along. Explain any unfamiliar words. Ask students to reread the letter silently, then answer questions 1–5. Correct the first four answers, then let students compare their choice of advice. Read Dot's answer together. Let students tell why they agree or disagree with Dot's solution and perhaps offer some other solutions.

63

Forms of the Simple Present Tense

I
You
We
They ⎬ work.

I
You
We
They ⎬ *work* at a restaurant.
study English.
teach English.
fix cars.

Look at each picture. Learn the job name. Then write what the people do, using the simple present tense. Use the Data Bank to help you.

1. I'm a musician.

I play in an

orchestra.

2. I'm a pilot.

_____

3. I'm a builder.

_____

4. We are waiters.

_____

5. We are mechanics.

_____

6. We are nurses.

_____

7. They are architects.

_____

8. They are mail carriers.

_____

9. They are custodians.

_____

DATA BANK

We serve food in a restaurant.	We take care of sick people.	They deliver mail to homes.
They draw plans for buildings.	I fly airplanes.	They clean school buildings.
I build houses.	~~I play in an orchestra.~~	We fix cars and trucks.

SKILL OBJECTIVES: Building vocabulary; using simple present tense. Teach/review the vocabulary and call attention to the box at the top of the page. Then have volunteers make sentences for each of the nine items. Call attention to the Data Bank before assigning this as independent written work.

More Occupations

More Forms of the Simple Present Tense		
He She } works. It	(When the subject is *he, she,* or *it* or the name of a person or thing, add *-s* or *-es* to the verb.)	He *works* in a shop. It *rains* every spring. Jan *fixes* cars.

Look at each picture. Learn the job name. Then write what the people do, using the simple present tense. Use the Data Bank to help you.

1. He is a reporter.

 He writes stories for
 newspapers and TV.

2. She is a farmer.

_____

_____

3. He is a teacher.

_____

_____

4. She is a photographer.

_____

_____

5. He is a chef.

_____

_____

6. She is a veterinarian.

_____

_____

7. She is a police officer.

_____

_____

8. He is an artist.

_____

_____

9. She is a bus driver.

_____

_____

DATA BANK		
drives a bus	~~writes stories for newspapers and TV~~	takes care of sick animals
cooks in a restaurant	and TV takes pictures with a camera	draws and paints pictures
teaches math	grows food for people to eat	gives traffic tickets

SKILL OBJECTIVES: Building vocabulary; using simple present tense. Call attention to the box at the top of the page and give several examples of the spelling and pronunciation of the *s/es* forms. You may want to devise a list of verbs with different *s/z/es* endings, such as *drives* (z), *paints* (s), and *watches* (es). Teach/review the vocabulary, then have volunteers do the nine items orally. Monitor for correct pronunciation of verb endings. Call attention to the Data Bank. Then assign the page for independent written work.

A Busy Family

Read the story.

The Watsons

The Watsons work hard. Mr. Watson is an architect. Mrs. Watson is a teacher. They have two daughters. The oldest, Lisa Watson, is a dentist. Her sister, Rosa Watson, is a police officer.

Mr. and Mrs. Watson have a son, Mike. He works hard at school. He wants to be an architect, like his father.

Mr. Watson's mother lives with the Watsons. She is sixty-eight and is a retired chef. She is not a chef anymore. "Now I help my family out," she says. "Every day I cook dinner for my children and grandchildren."

A **Answer the following questions.**

1. Who in the Watson family draws plans for buildings?

   a. Mrs. Watson **b.** Mr. Watson **c.** Lisa Watson

2. Who in the Watson family teaches students?

   a. Mike Watson **b.** Rosa Watson **c.** Mrs. Watson

3. Who looks at people's teeth?

   a. Lisa Watson **b.** Mr. Watson **c.** Rosa Watson

4. Who gives tickets and arrests people who break the law?

   a. Mrs. Watson **b.** Rosa Watson **c.** Mr. Watson's mother

5. Who would like to be an architect someday?

   a. Mike Watson **b.** Mr. Watson **c.** Lisa Watson

6. What is true about Mr. Watson's mother?

   a. She was an architect. **b.** She was a dentist. **c.** She was a chef.

B **Read about the following people. Write the names of their jobs. Use the Data Bank to help you.**

1. I clean office buildings. _____

2. I deliver letters. _____

3. I play an instrument. _____

4. I fix machines. _____

DATA BANK

| mechanic | musician | mail carrier | custodian |

SKILL OBJECTIVES: Building vocabulary; making inferences. Have students read the story aloud. *Part A*: Do question 1 orally with the class. Ask them to tell why "Mr. Watson" is the answer. Then assign Part A for independent work. After the class has finished marking their answers, correct Part A, asking for reasons for each choice. *Part B*: Review the vocabulary in the Data Bank, then ask students to write their answers. Discuss what other things people in each occupation do (for example, mechanics fix car engines; musicians play in orchestras, bands, or as solo artists; mail carriers deliver letters and packages; custodians make small repairs in a building and monitor heating and cooling apparatuses).

How Much Do They Make?

This graph shows the approximate average annual salaries for people in various jobs. Be sure you understand the meanings of *approximate*, *average*, and *annual*. Read the graph and then do the exercises below it.

Language Objectives
Answer questions about people's salaries. Agree or disagree with statements about salaries.

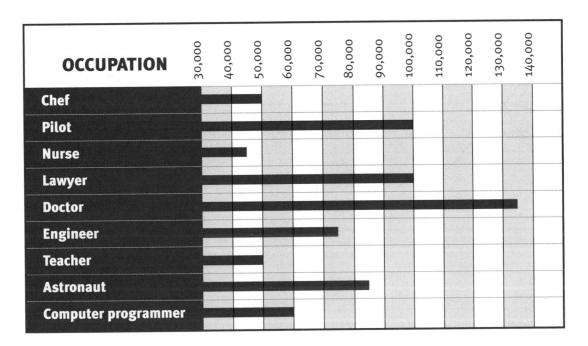

OCCUPATION	30,000	40,000	50,000	60,000	70,000	80,000	90,000	100,000	110,000	120,000	130,000	140,000
Chef		45,000										
Pilot								100,000				
Nurse	35,000											
Lawyer								100,000				
Doctor												140,000
Engineer					75,000							
Teacher			50,000									
Astronaut						85,000						
Computer programmer			50,000									

A Read the sentences below carefully and fill in the blanks. The first one is done for you.

1. The approximate average salary for engineers is _____$75,000_____ a year.

2. Pilots are paid about $ _____ a year.

3. The average doctor earns about $ _____ annually.

4. Astronauts get paid approximately $ _____ each year.

5. The average annual pay for teachers is about $ _____.

6. Chefs in restaurants have an annual salary of about $ _____.

7. Nurses receive about $ _____ each year.

B Read these sentences. Answer with *Yes* or *No*.

1. A teacher's average salary is more than a pilot's. _____

2. A doctor's salary is about $135,000 a year. _____

3. Astronauts and doctors have about the same average salaries. _____

4. An engineer's average salary is less than a teacher's. _____

5. The average annual salary of nurses is more than $40,000. _____

6. A chef's average salary is about $70,000 a year. _____

SKILL OBJECTIVES: Reading a bar graph; understanding *more than/less than*. Read the directions aloud. Explain any unfamiliar words. Go over the data shown on the graph. For each occupation, ask, "What is the ...'s salary?" *Part A:* Do the first example with the students. Show how the answer is read from the graph. Then assign the remaining items. *Part B:* Teach the phrases and concepts *more than* and *less than*. Ask, "Which salaries are more/less than the (pilot's) salary?" After sufficient oral practice, assign Part B for independent work. Correct and discuss the page with the class. If appropriate, have students research other salaries and graph them.

Interviewing: Personal Preferences

Language Objective
Ask questions and record information.

A Interview people in your school. Ask these questions. Write their answers in the chart.

What's your name?   What's your favorite song?

How old are you?   What's your favorite color?

What do you want to be?   What's your favorite food?

Name	Age	Occupation	Favorite song	Favorite color	Favorite food

B Write a paragraph about some of the people above.

_____

_____

_____

_____

_____

_____

_____

_____

SKILL OBJECTIVES: Using a chart; writing a paragraph. Draw the chart from Part A on the board. Have students ask one volunteer student the questions from the top of the page. Show students how to fill out their own charts. Repeat this activity, then allow time for students to interview and chart independently. *Part B:* Have students help you build a paragraph, using the information from the board chart. (Example: *Stella is fifteen years old. She wants to be a pilot. Her favorite song is "What a Wonderful World." Her favorite color is red. Her favorite food is macaroni and cheese.*) You may wish to have students review the sample paragraph on page 119 before they write their own.

Where Are You From?

Language Objectives
Match a country with its primary language. Write informational sentences about people.

A Match the countries and nationalities. Write the letter of the nationality next to the name of the country it goes with.
The first one is done for you.

Country		Nationality
1. England	j	**a.** Peruvian
2. Ireland	_____	**b.** Brazilian
3. Laos	_____	**c.** Swiss
4. Japan	_____	**d.** Puerto Rican
5. Canada	_____	**e.** Vietnamese
6. Peru	_____	**f.** Turkish
7. Mexico	_____	**g.** Lebanese
8. Vietnam	_____	**h.** Japanese
9. United States	_____	**i.** Thai
10. Colombia	_____	**j.** English
11. Brazil	_____	**k.** Indian
12. Turkey	_____	**l.** American
13. China	_____	**m.** Mexican
14. Puerto Rico	_____	**n.** Chinese
15. Spain	_____	**o.** Laotian
16. Lebanon	_____	**p.** Greek
17. Thailand	_____	**q.** Irish
18. India	_____	**r.** Spanish
19. Switzerland	_____	**s.** Canadian
20. Greece	_____	**t.** Colombian

B Fill in the chart with any information you want. Then write sentences about these people in your notebook. See the example below.

Amin is from Lebanon. His native language is Arabic. He is a banker. He is 36 years old.

Name	Amin	Maria	Sue-Ling	Cristos	Hiro/Yoko	My Teacher	I
Country	Lebanon		China		Japan	?	?
Native language	Arabic	Spanish		Greek			
Occupation	banker		chemist				
Age	36				22/24		

SKILL OBJECTIVES: Naming countries and nationalities; completing a chart. Display a world map. Have students locate each country listed in Part A. Then ask, "What do we call people from (Vietnam)?" "Is anyone in this class from Vietnam?" ("Yes, Binh is Vietnamese.") Provide vocabulary as needed for students whose countries are not listed. *Part B:* Students are to fill in the missing information with any appropriate words. Do "Maria" with the class; then have the class write a sentence about her. When you are sure students understand the instructions, assign the page for independent work.

A New Career

Read the story.

Ricardo Estrada is from Quito, Ecuador. Ecuador is a country in South America. Now Ricardo lives in the United States. He lives in Boston.

Ricardo works in a restaurant. He is a chef. Someday he would like to own his own restaurant. He would like to be the restaurant's chef, too, because he enjoys cooking. He is also taking business classes. "It takes a lot of hard work to own your own business," he says. "You really have to know what you are doing. Someday I know I can have my own restaurant."

A **Complete the following sentences. Circle your answers.**

1. Ricardo is from
   a. Brazil.   **b.** Ireland.   **c.** Ecuador.

2. Ecuador is in
   a. South America.   **b.** Texas.   **c.** the United States.

3. Ricardo works as a
   a. pilot.   **b.** waiter.   **c.** chef.

4. Ricardo
   a. goes to school.   **b.** lives in Ecuador.   **c.** works as a veterinarian.

B **Ricardo wants to be a chef and the owner of a restaurant because he likes to cook. Match the following likes or interests and careers. The first one is done for you.**

Likes/Interests		Careers
1. flying airplanes	_d_	**a.** bus driver
2. serving food to people	_____	**b.** builder
3. driving buses	_____	**c.** artist
4. teaching others about different subjects	_____	**d.** pilot
5. painting pictures	_____	**e.** teacher
6. making sure people obey laws	_____	**f.** police officer
7. constructing buildings	_____	**g.** waiter/waitress

SKILL OBJECTIVES: Reading for details; making inferences; developing career vocabulary. Read the story aloud or have one or more volunteers read it. Review/introduce new vocabulary. Display a world map and have students find Ecuador. If you have students from Ecuador, have them tell about it. *Part A:* Do the first item orally with the class, then have them complete the others independently. *Part B:* Read over the instructions with the students and be sure they understand the connection between one's interests and one's possible occupational choices. Do item 1 orally. Then have them complete the page independently.

My Country and Yours: Writing a Description

Read the story.

Ireland is a small country in the North Atlantic Ocean. It is near the United Kingdom. Ireland is famous for many things. It is famous for its green country-side. In some parts of Ireland there are miles and miles of rolling, green fields. Other parts of Ireland are gray and rocky. Sometimes the weather in Ireland is chilly and damp. It rains a lot in Ireland; that's one reason the fields are so green.

Dublin is the capital of Ireland. Dublin is a beautiful old city. There are many small squares and parks in Dublin. O'Connell Street, in the center of Dublin, is very wide. There are fine stores on it. There is a very famous university in the city. It is called Trinity College.

The Irish people love to sing and dance and tell stories. It's a wonderful country.

United Kingdom

Ireland
★
Dublin

London
★

A   **Answer each of the questions below. Use short answers. The first one is done for you.**

1. Where is Ireland?   It's in the North Atlantic Ocean.

2. What country is Ireland near?   _____

3. What is the capital of Ireland?   _____

4. What university is in Dublin?   _____

5. What do the Irish love to do?   _____

B   **Write a paragraph about your country.**

_____
_____
_____
_____
_____
_____
_____
_____

SKILL OBJECTIVES: Reading for details; writing an informative essay. Read the section aloud as students follow along, or have volunteers read it. Explain unfamiliar words. Have students reread the text silently. Discuss some or all of the comprehension questions, then assign the page as independent writtem work. Students should use the text as a model as they write original essays about their native (or ancestral) countries. Allow time for students to read their essays aloud to the class.

Dear Dot

Dear Dot,

   This is my problem. I want to be an actor, but my father says, "No!" I want to take drama classes next year. My father says, "Take computer programming." I don't want to go to college. My father says, "Go to college. Get an education." My father is not a college graduate, so it is important to him. But I want to act, not study. What can I do?

                                                    Hamlet

1. What does Hamlet want to be? _____

2. What classes does he want to take? _____

3. What does his father want him to take? _____

4. Is his father a college graduate? _____

5. What is your advice for Hamlet? Circle your answer.

    a. Do what your father says.   **c.** Take both classes, if possible.

    b. Do what you want to do.   **d.** Leave home.

6. Now read Dot's answer. See if your answer is the same. If your answer is different, tell why you disagree. Dot's advice is below.

Dear Hamlet,
Listen to your father. Take computer programming and drama. Today you want to be an actor. Tomorrow you may want to be an accountant. Remember, most actors go to college nowadays. The more you know, the better off you are. Good luck.
Dot

A Fill in the missing word. The first two are done for you.

1. There _____*is*_____ one airport in Boston.

2. There _____*are*_____ ten students in the class.

3. There _____ a few cars in the parking lot.

4. There _____ a letter on the table for you.

5. There _____ many universities in Dallas.

6. There _____ a big park in this city.

B Write the negative sentence. Then write the question. The first one is done for you.

1. There are three banks on Main Street.

   Negative: ___There aren't any banks on Main Street.___

   Question: ___Are there any banks on Main Street?___

2. There are a few letters on the desk.

   Negative: _____

   Question: _____

3. There are two hospitals in Montclair.

   Negative: _____

   Question: _____

4. There are several students from Mexico in my class.

   Negative: _____

   Question: _____

C Write the question that goes with each answer. The first one is done for you.

1. There are fifteen hospitals in Fort Worth.

   Question: ___How many hospitals are there in Fort Worth?___

2. There are fourteen students from Vietnam in my school.

   Question: _____

3. There are more than ten million people in Los Angeles.

   Question: _____

Plurals: More than One

Plural means more than one. Read the rules for spelling plural words.

Rule	Singular	Plural
Add -s to most nouns.	book boy	books boys
Change -y nouns to -ies if -y follows a consonant.*	city	cities
Add -es to -ss, -sh, -ch, and -x nouns.	class dish watch box	classes dishes watches boxes

* Consonants: b c d f g h j k l m n p q r s t v w x y
** Vowels: a e i o u

Rule	Singular	Plural
Add -es to -o nouns if -o follows a consonant.*	potato tomato	potatoes tomatoes
Add -s to -o nouns if -o follows a vowel.**	radio	radios
Exceptions	child man woman foot mouse tooth	children men women feet mice teeth

A Write the plural form of each word. The first one is done for you.

1. egg ___eggs___
2. shoe _____
3. country _____
4. church _____
5. bridge _____
6. hotel _____
7. blouse _____
8. chair _____
9. taxi _____
10. peach _____
11. doctor _____
12. suit _____
13. tooth _____
14. shirt _____
15. student _____
16. berry _____

17. name _____
18. man _____
19. daughter _____
20. banana _____
21. orange _____
22. baby _____
23. apple _____
24. nurse _____
25. jacket _____
26. lawyer _____
27. stool _____
28. woman _____
29. pilot _____
30. foot _____
31. child _____
32. hat _____

33. secretary _____
34. letter _____
35. friend _____
36. belt _____
37. book _____
38. library _____
39. radio _____
40. brother _____
41. brush _____
42. sandwich _____
43. dog _____
44. carrot _____
45. cemetery _____
46. rug _____
47. family _____
48. cousin _____

B Choose twenty-five of these words you know well. Write a sentence for each one. Underline the plurals you use in the sentence.

For example: *My <u>friends</u> are coming to town.*

SKILL OBJECTIVES: Learning spelling rules for forming plurals; writing original sentences. Read and discuss as necessary the rules in the boxes. *Part A*: Do the first ten examples as a group activity, reviewing the applicable rules and the pronunciations. Then assign the page as independent written work. After students have completed Part B, ask each one to read his or her favorite sentence aloud.

74

What's Happening at School Today?

A Read the sentences carefully. Then write the number of the sentence next to the picture it describes. The first one is done for you.

1. In one classroom, a girl is sharpening a pencil.

2. In the gym, students are exercising.

3. In the hall, a boy is opening his locker.

4. In one classroom, two girls are whispering.

5. In the home economics class, students are cooking.

6. In the cafeteria, two boys are fighting.

7. In one classroom, a boy is goofing off.

8. In the hall, a boy is getting a drink.

B Write about the picture in your notebook. You may use the sentences above or make up sentences of your own. Start with the following title and topic sentence.

One Day at Park Junior High

It's a busy day at Park Junior High School.

DATA BANK			
cooking	getting a drink	sharpening a pencil	exercising
fighting	goofing off	opening his locker	whispering

SKILL OBJECTIVES: Present progressive; writing a paragraph. Teach/review the words and phrases in the Data Bank. Ask volunteers to pantomime specific actions. Ask, "What is/are (he/she/they) doing?" Reinforce as many phrases as possible this way. Have students search the picture to answer two questions about each Data Bank word or phrase: "Who is (cooking)?" "Where is/are (he/she/they) (cooking)?" Teach necessary vocabulary (home economics class, etc.). Students may read the sentences aloud, then complete the page independently.

Interviewing: This School

Language Objectives
Ask questions and record information. Write a paragraph using the collected information.

A Interview your teachers, the school secretary, or the assistant principal to find out the answers to these questions.

1. How many students are there in this school? _____

2. How many students are there from Mexico? _____

3. How many classrooms are there? _____

4. How many teachers are there? _____

5. How many librarians are there? _____

6. How many guidance counselors are there? _____

7. How many buses are there? _____

8. Are there any TVs in the school? _____

9. Are there any computers? _____

10. Are there any students from Vietnam? _____

B Now write a paragraph about your school.

Here are some interesting facts about my school. _____

_____

_____

_____

_____

_____

_____

_____

_____

_____

SKILL OBJECTIVES: *There is/are;* **interviewing; writing a paragraph.** If possible, ask the principal, assistant principal, or school secretary to visit your class armed with the necessary statistics. If this is not possible, research these questions yourself, and let the class interview you. Have students use the information to make oral statements about their school. Example: "There are … students in this school" Then assign Part B as independent written work. Students may refer to the sample paragraph on page 119 for format if they need to.

76

Reading a Chart

The following chart shows the nationality and the native language of students at Central School. Read the chart and look at the box under it.

Language Objective
Answer questions using numbers and quantifiers a <u>few</u> and <u>many</u>.

Country of Origin	Native Language	Number of Students
Dominican Republic	Spanish	34
Mexico	Spanish	101
Guatemala	Spanish	56
Puerto Rico	Spanish	34
Vietnam	Vietnamese	21
Haiti	French	12
Lebanon	Arabic	4
Korea	Korean	3
Japan	Japanese	1

There is …	(used when talking about one thing or person)
There are …	(used when talking about more than one thing or person)
There are a few.	(used when talking about a small number)
There are many.	(used when talking about a large number)

A Answer these questions. Use complete sentences. The first one is done for you.

1. How many Mexicans are there in this school?   *There are 101 Mexicans.*

2. How many Haitians are there?   _____

3. How many Spanish speakers are there?   _____

4. How many Vietnamese are there?   _____

5. How many Japanese are there?   _____

6. How many students are there all together?   _____

B Now answer these questions. The first two are done for you.

1. Are there any students from Korea?   *Yes, there are a few.*

2. Are there any students from China?   *No, there aren't any.*

3. Are there any students from Mexico?   _____

4. Are there any students from Lebanon?   _____

5. Are there any students from Spain?   _____

6. Are there any Dominicans?   _____

SKILL OBJECTIVES: *There is/are*; finding information from a chart. Have students read the data on the chart aloud. Read the box under the chart with the students and make sure they understand both concepts: when to use *there is* and when to use *there are*; and when to use *there are few* and when to use *there are many*. Go through all the items in Parts A and B orally before assigning the page as independent written work.

Reading a Pie Chart

Pie charts are often used to show percents. This pie chart shows the native language of students at the El Rancho School. Use the chart to answer the questions.

El Rancho School: Native Language of Students

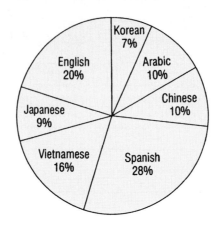

A Answer these questions. The first one is done for you.

1. What percent (%) of the students speak Japanese as their native language? _9%_

2. What percent speak Korean as their native language? _____

3. What percent speak Vietnamese as their native language? _____

4. What percent come from families whose native language is not English? _____

B Read these statements and put a *T* in the blank if the statement is true, an *F* if the statement is false, and a *?* if the chart doesn't give you the information. The first two are done for you.

1. There are more Spanish speakers at this school than any other group. _T_

2. Most of the Spanish speakers are from Mexico. _?_

3. There are more Chinese-speaking students than Japanese-speaking students. _____

4. There are as many Arabic speakers as there are Korean speakers. _____

5. Only a few of the Chinese speakers are from Hong Kong. _____

6. There are more students whose native language is Vietnamese than there are whose native language is English. _____

7. There are more whose native language is English than any other group. _____

8. 42% of the students are from Asian countries (Korea, Japan, Vietnam, and China). _____

C In your notebook, write one or more sentences telling why you think this type of chart is called a "pie" chart.

SKILL OBJECTIVES: Interpreting a pie chart; answering true/false questions; making inferences. Read the directions aloud to the students. Review the meaning of "percent." Have students read the title above the pie chart; be sure they understand what is meant by "native language." Review the concepts of "more than" and "as many as." Work through all the questions in Parts A and B before assigning the page as independent work.

San Diego Outdoor Markets

Language Objective
Agree or disagree about statements in a reading.

Read the article.

San Diego is a beautiful city. It is located on the coast of California, beside the Pacific Ocean. It has mountains nearby.

There are many things to do in San Diego. You can go to its famous zoo. You can walk by the harbor. You can surf in the ocean's waves. You can also go to one of the city's many outdoor markets. San Diego is famous for its farmer's markets. You can find these markets all over the city all year round. This is because the weather is usually warm and pleasant in San Diego. Crops grow well in weather that is warm all year round.

Many farmers have farms near San Diego. Once a week, they bring their products—from fresh tomatoes to juicy oranges to tasty grapes—into the city to be sold. One well-known farmer's market is the Horton Square market. It takes place every Thursday afternoon.

There is also a popular flower market at Horton Square. You can buy beautiful red, orange, and yellow tropical flowers. Or you can buy bright white orchids. You might buy a flowering plant for inside your house. Or you might buy a bouquet as a gift. San Diego is called the flower capital of the United States. It's a wonderful city to live in.

Read each sentence below. Write *T* if the sentence is true. Write *F* if the sentence is false. Write *?* if the answer is impossible to know. The first one is done for you.

1. San Diego is near the Pacific Ocean. _____T_____

2. People like living in San Diego. _____

3. There is not much to do in San Diego. _____

4. San Diego has a nice harbor. _____

5. San Diego's farmer's markets are famous. _____

6. The farmer's markets are only open for part of the year. _____

7. San Diego has many days of nice weather during the year. _____

8. Crops grow well in any weather. _____

9. Farmers often bring goods from outside California. _____

10. The Horton Square farmer's market happens on Thursdays. _____

11. You can find tomatoes at San Diego farmer's markets. _____

12. The Horton Square flower market sells no tropical flowers. _____

13. San Diego is called the flower capital of the United States. _____

14. Everyone in San Diego likes flowers. _____

SKILL OBJECTIVE: Reading for details. Read the article aloud as students follow along (San Diego in California is pronounced SAN dee-AY-goh). Explain unfamiliar vocabulary. Have students locate San Diego on a United States map. Then write these sentences on the board: *San Diego is a city in California. Horton Square is in Philadelphia. The Horton Square flower market is expensive.* Have the students decide which statement is true, which is false, and which is impossible to know from reading the story. Ask students to reread the article silently before completing the page independently.

Philadelphia: Facts and Opinions

Language Objective
Distinguish between fact and opinion.

Read the story.

When Mr. Jenkins visits a city, he likes riding the bus. Today, he is riding across Philadelphia. He wants to see as much of the city as he can. His bus driver likes to talk. The driver is talking to Mr. Jenkins.

"So this is your first time in Philadelphia? Philadelphia is terrific. I have lived here for twenty years. You can do all kinds of things here. A lot of people like to go downtown and see the Liberty Bell. It's amazing! They rang it the first time the Declaration of Independence was read out loud. People also like to go and see Independence Hall. That's where the Declaration of Independence was approved. One draft of the Constitution was also written there.

"Another nice spot is Betsy Ross's house. Do you know who Betsy Ross is? The story about her is that she made the first American flag. But maybe it's just a story.

"If you like art, try the Philadelphia Art Museum! It's full of beautiful paintings. There's also the Barnes Collection, but that is not as good as the Art Museum.

"The Philadelphia Zoo is the oldest zoo in the country. It's also the best. Their exhibits are really amazing, and they have more wild animals than you could ever believe!"

The bus driver is giving Mr. Jenkins a lot of information at once. Many things the driver says are *facts*. Facts are true statements that you can read or check in an encyclopedia or other reference book. Other things the driver says are *opinions*. Opinions are what a person thinks about something. They are true for the person saying them, but they are not true for everyone. You cannot check them in a reference book. Two people can have completely different *opinions* about the same *facts*.

Look at each sentence below. If it is a fact, write *Fact* next to it. If it is an opinion, write *Opinion* next to it. The first one is done for you.

1. The bus driver has lived in Philadelphia for twenty years. _____Fact_____

2. The Liberty Bell is beautiful. _____

3. The Declaration of Independence was approved at Independence Hall. _____

4. Betsy Ross's house is a nice spot. _____

5. Betsy Ross may have made the first American flag. _____

6. The Philadelphia Art Museum has beautiful paintings. _____

7. The Barnes Collection is an art museum in Philadelphia. _____

8. The Philadelphia Art Museum is better than the Barnes Collection. _____

9. The Philadelphia Zoo is the oldest zoo in the country. _____

10. The exhibits at the Philadelphia Zoo are amazing. _____

SKILL OBJECTIVE: Distinguishing between fact and opinion. Read the story aloud as students follow along. Have students locate Philadelphia on a United States map. Read the explanation of the difference between a fact and an opinion. Write the following sentences on the board: *Philadelphia is the capital of Pennsylvania. Philadelphia is terrific.* Let students decide which is a fact and which is an opinion, then explain their reasons. Have students reread the story before completing the *Fact vs. Opinion* exercise. Let students compare and discuss their answers.

Miami: the Main Idea

Language Objectives
Answer questions about a reading. Write questions for specific statements. Write about a city.

Read the article.

Miami is a big city in Florida. It borders the Atlantic Ocean and is also where the Miami River joins the sea. There are many interesting things to do in and around Miami. Because the average temperature in Miami is a comfortable 75 degrees Fahrenheit, vacationers and people who live in Miami year-round go to the beaches frequently. The famous Miami Beach is just east of Miami. Some people in the northern states who want to escape the cold winters spend a month or more in Miami Beach.

Miami is not far from Everglades National Park, a huge, swampy nature preserve. Visitors can see wetland wildlife in the Everglades.

A Miami vacation can also include a trip to Biscayne National Park on Biscayne Bay. There, you can swim in the ocean, or you can take a tour on a glass-bottomed boat that lets you see many different kinds of fish.

Nearby is the Miami Seaquarium. You can learn about such remarkable sea mammals as dolphins and killer whales there. The Seaquarium is home to endangered sea turtles. They are in danger of disappearing in the wild. The Seaquarium gives them a safe place to live.

A **What is the main idea of this article? Circle the right answer.**

a. Miami is near the Everglades.

b. There are beaches near Miami.

c. You can find sea turtles at the Miami Seaquarium.

d. There are interesting things to do in and around Miami, Florida.

B **Write questions to go with the answers.**

1. _____? A huge, swampy nature preserve.

2. _____? It is on Biscayne Bay.

3. _____? Dolphins and killer whales.

4. _____? It lets you see many fish up close.

5. _____? Just east of Miami.

6. _____? It is 75 degrees Fahrenheit.

C **Write a name for the story.**

_____

D **In your notebook, write a short essay about a city you know. Use the reading above as a model. Use the Internet or an encyclopedia for research, if necessary.**

SKILL OBJECTIVE: Identifying the main idea; making inferences; forming questions. Read the article aloud. Explain any new words. Have students locate Miami on a map. Write on the board, *What…? Where…? Which…? Why…?* Have students use these forms to ask questions about the selection. *Part A:* Have students compare their answers and discuss why only one choice states the main idea. If you wish, do Parts B and C as group activities before assigning them as written work. *Part D:* Encourage students to write about a city they know well. Outline the model reading at the top of the page with students so they understand what kind of information to put in their essays.

Using a Pay Phone

Look at the pictures.

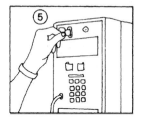   

A **Write the missing word. The first one is done for you.**

1. The woman is _____*entering*_____ the phone booth.

2. She is _____ a number in the phone book.

3. She is _____ the number.

4. She is _____ the phone.

5. She is _____ a coin or coins.

6. She is _____ the number.

7. She is _____ to someone.

8. She is _____ the phone.

DATA BANK			
talking	dialing	hanging up	picking up
looking for	writing down	depositing	~~entering~~

B **Think of an activity similar to using a pay phone. Write down all the steps in the activity, then demonstrate for the class. Tell what you are doing in each step. Use one of the examples below or think of your own activity.**

DATA BANK		
clearing the dinner table	giving a baby a bath	preparing for a test
making microwave popcorn	preparing a salad	fixing a flat tire

SKILL OBJECTIVES: Following and naming a sequence; using present progressive. Teach/review the vocabulary in the Data Bank. Have a student read one word or phrase. A second student will say the number of the matching picture. A third student will put the word(s) into a complete sentence. Example: "Talking." "Number 7," "She is talking (on the phone) to someone." Repeat this activity for all eight phrases. Provide vocabulary help as needed. *Part B:* Encourage students to think of as many steps as possible to describe their activity. Have each student present his/her sequence to the class.

Dear Dot

Language Objectives

Answer questions about a reading. Give advice. Agree or disagree with advice.

Dear Dot,

I am Vietnamese. There are no other Vietnamese kids in my school. I don't fit in here. I still don't speak English very well, and I feel stupid when I make mistakes. There are some girls I want to know, but I am too shy to talk to them. I am not happy, and I miss my country. What can I do?

Homesick and Sad

1. Where is the student from? _____

2. How many Vietnamese students are there in her school? _____

3. What language is she learning? _____

4. When does she feel stupid? _____

5. Who does she want to know? _____

6. What is your advice for Homesick and Sad? Circle your answer.

   a. Learn more English and make more friends.   **c.** Go back to your own country.

   b. Get a job.   **d.** Read more and watch television.

7. Now read Dot's answer. See if your answer is the same. If your answer is different, tell why you disagree. Dot's advice is below.

> Dear Homesick and Sad,
>
> Join a club or another kind of extra-curricular activity. Invite the girls you want to know to your house. Don't be so shy—ask them to help you practice your English. Teach them some words in Vietnamese. Then they will understand how hard English can be for you. Don't be afraid to ask for more help from other students and your teachers. Most people are happy to help if they know what your problem is.
>
> Dot

SKILL OBJECTIVES: Reading comprehension; making judgments. Read the letter aloud or have a volunteer read it as students follow along. Explain any unfamiliar words. Ask students to reread the letter silently, then answer questions 1–6. Correct the first five answers, then let students compare their choice of advice. Read Dot's answer together. Let students tell why they agree or disagree with Dot's solution and perhaps offer some different suggestions of their own.

What time is it? Write the sentence. The first one is done for you.

1. It's twenty to three.

2. _____

3. _____

4. _____

5. _____

6. _____

7. _____

8. _____

9. _____

10. _____

11. _____

12. _____

13. _____

14. _____

15. _____

16. _____

SKILL OBJECTIVE: Telling time to the nearest five minutes. Go over this page as an oral group activity. Name a clock by its number and ask a student to tell the time. Give all students a chance to respond at least once to the question, "What time is it?" For further practice, state a time and have the students identify, by number, the correct clock. After sufficient oral practice, assign the page for independent written work.

Time Zones

Look at the time zones on the U.S. map.

Language Objective
Answer questions about time zones.

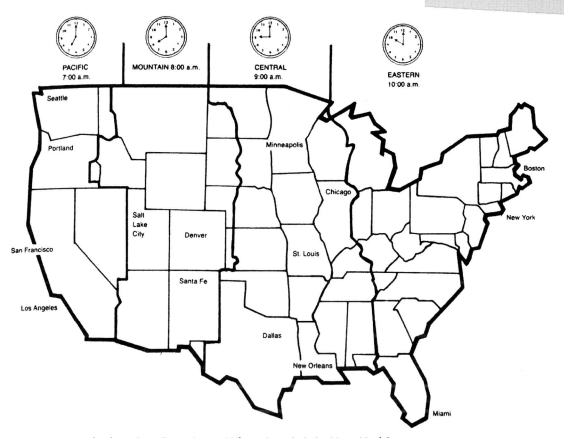

1. It's seven o'clock in San Francisco. What time is it in New York?

   It's ten o'clock in New York.

2. It's nine o'clock in Dallas. What time is it in Santa Fe?

   _____

3. It's ten o'clock in Miami. What time is it in Denver?

   _____

4. It's eight o'clock in Denver. What time is it in Salt Lake City?

   _____

5. If it is noon in Boston, what time is it in Los Angeles?

   _____

6. If it is noon in Chicago, what time is it in Seattle?

   _____

7. If it is noon in Minneapolis, what time is it in New Orleans?

   _____

8. If it is one p.m. in St. Louis, what time is it in Boston?

   _____

SKILL OBJECTIVES: Interpreting a map; computing time zone differences. Study the map with the class. If applicable, have students locate and plot their city or town on the map. Point out the four time zones. (Explain that there are additional time zones for eastern Canada, Alaska, and Hawaii.) Using the map, ask, for each city, "What time is it in …?" Next, write the actual time on the board (rounded to the nearest hour). Say, "It's … o'clock here. What time is it in …?" When the class shows understanding of the concept, assign the page for independent written work.

Where Are They Going?

Language Objective
Answer questions about daily activities.

Where's Peter going?		He's going to the bus station.
Why?		He's going to meet a friend.
When is he coming back?		He's coming back at 9:00.

A **Look at the pictures. Answer the questions.**

1. Where's he going? _____

2. Why? _____

3. When is he coming back? _____

4. Where are they going? _____

5. Why? _____

6. When are they coming back? _____

7. Where's she going? _____

8. Why? _____

9. When is she coming back? _____

B **Write sentences from this chart in your notebook.**

Example: Lisa is going to the library this afternoon.
She's going to return a book.

	Who	Where	When	Why
1.	Lisa	library	this afternoon	return a book
2.	Rob	music store	tonight	buy a CD
3.	I	cafeteria	now	have lunch
4.	Henry and Elena	airport	tomorrow	take a trip

SKILL OBJECTIVES: Using present progressive as future; using *going to* future; making inferences. Study the example box with the class. Be sure students understand how to use information in the picture clues. *Part A:* Work through Part A as an oral group activity. Answers to "Why?" should vary and provide a springboard for discussion about the different reasons people go to different places. *Part B:* Be sure students understand the instructions for Part B. Go over the example, showing how each part of each sentence comes directly from the chart. Then assign the page as independent written work.

Pronouns

A Finish these conversations. Fill in the missing words.

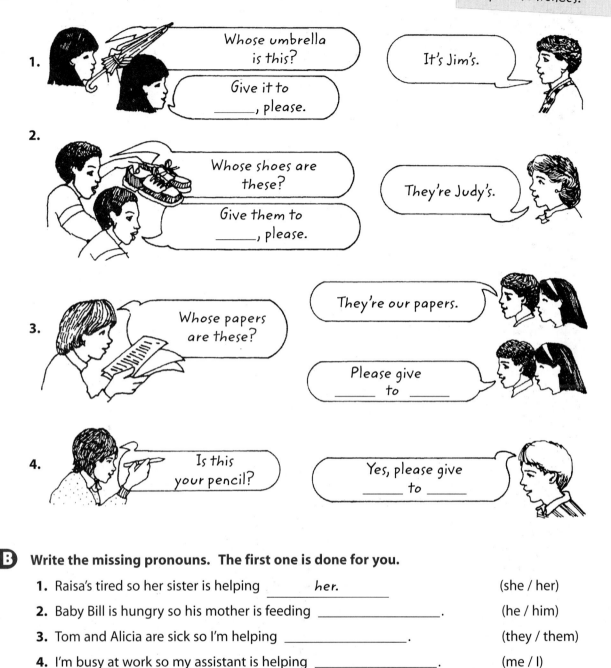

1. Whose umbrella is this?
   Give it to _____, please.

   It's Jim's.

2. Whose shoes are these?
   Give them to _____, please.

   They're Judy's.

3. Whose papers are these?

   They're our papers.

   Please give _____ to _____

4. Is this your pencil?

   Yes, please give _____ to _____

B Write the missing pronouns. The first one is done for you.

1. Raisa's tired so her sister is helping _____*her.*_____   (she / her)

2. Baby Bill is hungry so his mother is feeding _____.   (he / him)

3. Tom and Alicia are sick so I'm helping _____.   (they / them)

4. I'm busy at work so my assistant is helping _____.   (me / I)

5. You are tired so we are helping _____.   (us / you)

6. We are busy so our friends are helping _____.   (us / we)

7. My dog is hungry so I'm feeding _____.   (it's / it)

8. My clothes are dirty so I'm washing _____.   (they / them)

9. Our stove is dirty so my brother is cleaning _____.   (them / it)

10. My car is broken so I'm fixing _____.   (its / it)

SKILL OBJECTIVE: Using pronouns and possessives. Write these sentences on the board: *Give the book to Ann. Give the money to Jim and Ed. Give the cards to Maria and me.* Underline the direct object. Have a student repeat each sentence using the pronoun replacement. ("Give *it* to Ann.") Underline the indirect object. Have a student substitute both pronouns. ("Give *it* to *her.*") Then ask, "Whose book is it?" ("It's Ann's.") Have students read and complete Part A orally. Do some or all of Part B orally before assigning the pages as independent written work.

Going Places

**Read each paragraph carefully. Where are the people going?
Write the name of the place.**

1. Many people are going here this morning. They are going to deposit money and cash checks. Where are these people going?

   _____

2. Other people are going here. They are going to sit on the sand, swim, and dive. Where are they going?

   _____

3. At this place people are going to go to class, to the library, to meet their friends, and to study. Where are they going?

   _____

4. At this place, people are going to read, borrow and return books, and use the Internet. Where are they going?

   _____

5. Some people are going here to pick up packages. Others are going to mail letters and to buy stamps. Where are all these people going?

   _____

6. At this place people are going to buy drinks and candy, eat popcorn, and watch a film. Where are they going?

   _____

7. Many people are going here today. Some are going to buy meat and cheese. Others are buying milk and vegetables. Where are these people going?

   _____

8. At this place, people are going to buy flowers, visit sick friends, get X-rays and prescriptions. Where are they going?

   _____

9. Some people are going here to meet friends. Other people are going on vacations. They are all going to see many large planes. Where are these people going?

   _____

10. People are going here in their cars. They are going to buy gasoline and fill their tires with air. Some of them will talk to mechanics about their cars. Where are these people going?

    _____

DATA BANK

airport	beach	grocery store	library	post office
bank	gas station	hospital	movie theater	school

SKILL OBJECTIVES: Understanding uses of *going, going to*; drawing conclusions. Teach/review the vocabulary in the Data Bank. For each place, ask, "What do people do at/in a(n) …?" Do the first one or two examples as a group exercise, then assign the rest as independent written work.

A Ball Game in Chicago

Read the story.

Language Objective
Answer questions about a
reading. Write questions for
specific statements.

Larry and his dad are going to Chicago. They live in Saint Louis. They are going to take a train early Saturday morning. The night they arrive, they are going to see a baseball game.

Before they see the game, Larry and his dad are going to check into their hotel. They are going to have an early dinner, and then they are going to Wrigley Field. Wrigley Field is a very old baseball stadium. It was built in 1914!

The game Larry and his dad are going to see should be very exciting. The Chicago Cubs are playing the New York Mets. Larry and his dad are both big fans of the Cubs, one of the oldest baseball teams in the United States. The game is going to start at 8:00 p.m. It is going to be a nice night for a baseball game. The newspaper said the weather is going to be pleasant. When he goes to a game, Larry always likes to get peanuts. But he likes sitting with his dad and watching the game the most.

A **What is this story mostly about? Circle the answer.**

a. the history of Wrigley Field

b. the Chicago Cubs

c. the New York Mets

d. going to see a baseball game in Chicago

B **Answer these questions.**

1. How are Larry and his father going to Chicago? _____

_____

2. Where are Larry and his father staying in Chicago? _____

_____

3. When is the baseball game going to start? _____

_____

C **Write the questions. Then practice asking and answering with a classmate.**

1. _____ They are leaving on Saturday morning.

2. _____ They will see it the night they arrive.

3. _____ They are playing the New York Mets.

4. _____ It will start at 8:00 p.m.

SKILL OBJECTIVES: Identifying main idea; making inferences; asking questions. Read the text aloud as students follow along, or have a volunteer read it. Explain any new vocabulary. Have students reread the selection silently before answering the questions. Depending on the skill level of your group, you may wish to discuss the questions as a group before assigning as independent written work. If students work independently, be sure to discuss and compare answers after completion.

A Field Trip

Read the story.

Mrs. Horne's class is taking a field trip, and they can hardly wait! Mrs. Horne teaches social studies at a high school in Chevy Chase, Maryland. At the end of the week, she is taking her class on a field trip to Washington, D.C.

The class is going to see the Lincoln Memorial, built in memory of Abraham Lincoln, the United States' sixteenth president. It is a square structure, surrounded by thirty-six columns—the number of states in 1922.

Inside the memorial is a statue of Abraham Lincoln, nineteen feet high. On one wall, you can read the Gettysburg Address. The Gettysburg Address was a very famous speech by Lincoln.

Anyone visiting Washington, D.C. should see the Lincoln Memorial. It is a national treasure, a reminder that our freedoms cost the lives of the people who fought for them.

A **Answer the following questions. Use short answers.**

1. Where does Mrs. Horne teach?   _In Chevy Chase, Maryland._

2. Where is her class going?   _____

3. What is the class going to see?   _____

4. How many columns does the memorial have?   _____

5. What do the columns stand for?   _____

6. What is inside the memorial?   _____

7. What is on one wall of the memorial?   _____

8. What is the memorial a reminder of?   _____

_____

B **What is this story mostly about? Circle the correct answer.**

a. the Gettysburg address   c. Chevy Chase, Maryland

b. Mrs. Horne   d. the Lincoln Memorial

SKILL OBJECTIVE: **Identifying main idea and details.** Read the story aloud or have a volunteer read it. Explain unfamiliar words. Display a map of the United States. Help students locate Maryland and Washington, D.C. Explain to them that "D.C." stands for the District of Columbia, a place inside the state of Maryland. Ask students to reread the section silently before independently completing the page. Correct the students' answers together. Have students discuss their answer choice in Part B and explain why only answer d expresses the main idea of the story.

Dear Dot

Dear Dot

Dear Dot,
My problem is this: I like a girl in my class, but she doesn't know I exist. She is very popular. She is always going to a party or the movies or the mall with her girlfriends. I'm going to ask her out, but I'm very nervous. I don't know what to say or how to act. And what if she says no? I'm afraid of looking stupid.

Silent Admirer

1. Is the girl in the boy's class? _____

2. Is she popular? _____

3. What is he going to do? _____

4. What is he afraid of? _____

5. What is your advice for Silent Admirer? Circle your answer.

   a. Send her a letter.

   b. Ask one of her friends if she likes you.

   c. Be confident; don't worry about her answer.

   d. Forget about her; ask a different girl.

6. Now play the part of Dear Dot and write your own answer to Silent Admirer.

   Dear Silent Admirer, _____

   _____

   _____

   _____

   _____

   _____

   _____

   _____

   _____

   _____

SKILL OBJECTIVES: Reading comprehension; making judgments; writing a letter. Read the letter aloud as students follow along, or have a volunteer read it. Explain any unfamiliar words. Ask students to reread the letter silently and answer questions 1–5. Correct the first four answers, then let students compare their choice of advice. Finally, have students assume Dot's role and write a response in their own words. Help them with letter format, if necessary.

91

What Do You Have to Do?

Language Objective
Provide solutions to problems using _have to_ or _has to_.

A Bill has some problems. Write what he _has_ to do to solve his problems. The first one is done for you.

1. Bill's room is messy. _He has to clean his room._

2. The dishes are dirty. _____

3. His clothes are on the bed. _____

4. He is thirsty. _____

5. The waste baskets are full. _____

6. It's time for dinner. _____

7. The rugs are dirty. _____

8. The dog is hungry. _____

DATA BANK A

feed the dog	drink some water	wash the dishes	hang up his clothes
set the table	empty the waste baskets	vacuum the rugs	~~clean his room~~

B Here are some more problems. Write what the people _have_ to do to solve the problems. The first one is done for you.

Problems	**Solutions**
1. The students have a test tomorrow.	_They have to study._
2. My bike is broken.	_____
3. Susan is very sick.	_____
4. My father's birthday is tomorrow.	_____
5. There is no milk in my refrigerator.	_____
6. John is coming to a red light.	_____
7. My cousins are going to Paris soon.	_____
8. Our car is out of gas.	_____

DATA BANK B

call the doctor	buy some milk	buy a present	stop the car
get passports	go to a gas station	~~study~~	fix my bike

SKILL OBJECTIVES: Using _have to, has to_; drawing conclusions. _Part A:_ Teach/review the phrases in Data Bank A. Have a volunteer mime one of the actions. Ask the class, "What does (Luis) have to do?" ("He has to set the table.") Repeat for all eight expressions. Read the directions. Do one or two examples with the class, then have students work independently. _Part B:_ Teach/review vocabulary in Data Bank B. Do the exercise orally before assigning as independent written work. Listen for use of the correct pronoun and verb form.

Can and Can't

Language Objective
Tell what people can and can't do.

A Read the question and look at the picture. Then answer the question. The first one is done for you.

1. What sport can he play?

   He can play soccer.

2. What instrument can she play?

   _____

3. What game can they play?

   _____

4. What sport can you play?

   _____

5. What instrument can they play?

   _____

B Now write a story about yourself. What can you do? What can't you do?

_____

_____

_____

_____

_____

_____

_____

_____

_____

SKILL OBJECTIVES: Using modals *can, can't*; writing a story. *Part A:* Do this section as an oral group activity before assigning as independent written work. *Part B:* Write the following questions on the board: *What sports can you play? What games can you play? What instruments can you play? What languages can you speak? Can you ride a bike? Can you type? Can you make coffee?* Have students suggest other *Can you ...?* questions, then discuss what they can and can't do. Encourage students to read their finished stories aloud.

Interviewing: *Can You ... ?*

Language Objectives
Collect information. Present information to a group.

Interview two classmates. Write their names above the two columns. Then write their answers in the box. Report your findings to the class.

Things People Do	Name: Student 1	Student 2
1. Can you skate?		
2. Can you play the guitar?		
3. Can you dance?		
4. Can you play ping-pong?		
5. Can you run a mile?		
6. Can you speak Spanish?		
7. Can you play chess?		
8. Can you swim?		
9. Can you cook?		
10. Can you play the drums?		
11. Can you ski?		
12. Can you play soccer?		
13. Can you type?		
14. Can you drive?		
15. Can you ride a horse?		
16. Can you fix a car?		

SKILL OBJECTIVES: Using modals *can, can't*; interviewing; using a chart. Teach/review the vocabulary on the page, then divide the class into groups of four. Each student should interview two other students from his/her group.

A Bike Trip

Read the story.

Language Objective
Answer questions about a reading.

Beth is going on a ride on her mountain bike. She is going riding with her sister in the Squirrel Mountains. She's getting her bicycle ready for the long trip. She's polishing the handlebars. She's putting fresh grease on the chain. She's filling the tires with air. She's tightening the seat. Now she's ready to go.

This is Beth's first trip of the summer. She's a good rider. The Squirrel Mountains are twenty-five miles from Beth's house. Beth and her sister are going to stay there all day. At 5:30 they are going to ride home. It is going to be a wonderful day.

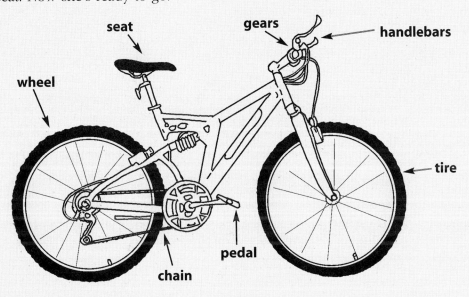

Answer these questions. The first one is done for you.

1. What is Beth going to do?   *She is going on a bike ride.*

2. Where is Beth riding? _____

3. Whom is Beth riding with? _____

4. What is Beth doing to the handlebars of her bike? _____

5. What is she doing to the chain? _____

6. What is she doing to the tires? _____

7. What is she doing to the seat? _____

8. How far away from Beth's house are the Squirrel Mountains? _____

_____

SKILL OBJECTIVES: Interpreting a diagram; reading for details. Study the mountain bicycle diagram with the class. Go over the labeled parts. Read the story aloud as students follow along, or have a volunteer read it. Explain any unfamiliar words. Point out that "bike" is another word for bicycle, and that gears change the speed at which the bicycle wheels turn.

Stacy's Car

Language Objectives
Associate driving activities with parts of a car. Write about a car.

Stacy has to drive to a friend's birthday party. This is the car she is driving.

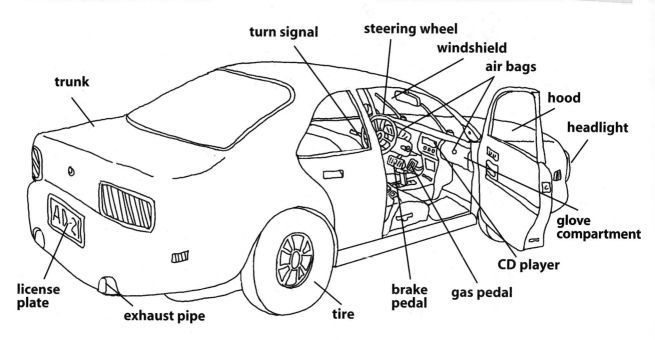

A In the column at the right are some parts of Stacy's car. Decide what each part does. Read the sentences on the left. Draw a line from the sentence to the part of the car Stacy will use. The first one is done for you.

1. Stacy is turning.

2. Stacy is going too fast.

3. Stacy listens to music.

4. Stacy wants to tell other drivers she is turning.

5. Stacy wants to put something away.

6. These protect Stacy in an accident.

7. Stacy looks under this to see the car's motor.

a. brake pedal

b. air bags

c. steering wheel

d. hood

e. turn signal

f. glove compartment

g. CD player

B In your notebook, write about the car you have or would someday like to have. Tell as much as you can about it. What kind is it? What color is it? Is it old or new? How big is it?

SKILL OBJECTIVES: Interpreting a diagram; making inferences; writing a paragraph. Study the car diagram with the class. Ask questions about the labeled parts: "When do you use the brake pedal? How do you clean the windshield? How do you speed up the car?" etc. *Part A:* Teach any new vocabulary, then assign for independent work. *Part B:* If possible, display magazine pictures of cars. If they wish, students may choose one of these pictures to describe.

Road Signs

Use words from the Data Bank to tell what the signs mean.
The first one is done for you.

1.

_____one way_____

_____

2.

_____

_____

3.

_____

_____

4.

_____

_____

5.

_____

_____

6.

_____

_____

7.

_____

_____

8.

_____

_____

9.

_____

_____

10.

_____

_____

11.

_____

_____

12.

_____

_____

DATA BANK

hospital	airport ahead	railroad crossing
intersection	phone ahead	school zone
no left turn	food ahead	slippery when wet
no parking	~~one way~~	two way traffic

SKILL OBJECTIVE: Interpreting road signs. Teach/review the vocabulary on this page. Let students independently write the correct term under each road sign. Correct and discuss the answers as a class.

More Road Signs

Circle the traffic rule that goes with each sign.
The first one is done for you.

a. You have to stop.
b. You can stop.
c. You can't stop.

a. You can't turn right.
b. You have to turn right.
c. You can turn right.

a. You can't ride your bike.
b. Be careful riding your bike.
c. You can ride your bike.

a. No parking before 8:30 a.m.
b. No parking after 5:30 p.m.
c. No parking between 8:30 a.m. and 5:30 p.m.

a. You can drive more than 55 mph.
b. You have to drive more than 55 mph.
c. You can't drive more than 55 mph.

a. You can get gas ahead.
b. You can't get gas ahead.
c. You have to get gas ahead.

a. You can enter this street.
b. Be careful entering this street.
c. You can't enter this street.

a. You can pass other cars.
b. You have to pass other cars.
c. You have to stay behind other cars.

a. There is a hospital ahead.
b. There is a hotel or motel ahead.
c. There is a bed ahead.

a. You can walk across this street.
b. You can't walk across this street.
c. Be careful walking across this street.

SKILL OBJECTIVES: Interpreting road signs; understanding modals *have to, can, can't*. Do the first one or two items as a group exercise. Be sure students understand the difference between *can* and *have to*. Emphasize the need to read each sentence carefully. Assign the page for independent work. Correct and discuss the answers together.

Dear Dot

Dear Dot,
   This is my problem. Ernesto, my brother, is good at everything. He can sing and dance and play the drums, and can speak <u>three</u> languages. Our friends call him "Ernesto the Great" or "Ernesto the Champ." I can write good stories, and I can play the guitar. How can I get people to pay attention to the things I am good at?

Little Brother Juan

1. What is Juan's problem? _____

_____

2. Name three things Ernesto can do. _____

_____

3. What can Juan do? _____

_____

4. Now write a letter to Little Brother Juan. Give him your advice. Tell him exactly what to do and what *not* to do.

   <u>Dear Juan,</u>

_____

_____

_____

_____

_____

_____

                                                    _____

SKILL OBJECTIVES: Reading comprehension; making judgments; writing a letter. Read the letter aloud as students follow along, or have a volunteer read it. Explain any unfamiliar words. Ask students to reread the letter silently, then answer questions 1–3. Correct their answers. Discuss possible answers to question 4 and then have students write their solutions.

Unit 11 Parts of the Body

Health, the Weather, and Social Engagements

Language Objective
Name parts of the body and common ailments.

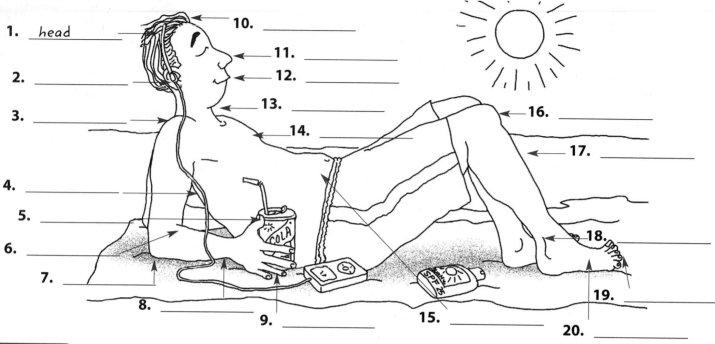

1. head
2. _____
3. _____
4. _____
5. _____
6. _____
7. _____
8. _____
9. _____
10. _____
11. _____
12. _____
13. _____
14. _____
15. _____
16. _____
17. _____
18. _____
19. _____
20. _____

A Write the name of each body part on the line. Use the words in Data Bank A. The first one is done for you.

DATA BANK A						
ankle	chest	finger	~~head~~	mouth	throat	wrist
arm	ear	foot	knee	nose	thumb	shoulder
back	elbow	hair	leg	stomach	toe	

B Use the words in Data Bank B to write a sentence about each person's problem.

1. She has a headache. 2. _____ 3. _____

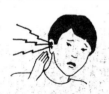 

4. _____ 5. _____ 6. _____

DATA BANK B					
~~stomachache~~	sore throat	earache	backache	headache	broken leg

SKILL OBJECTIVES: Building vocabulary; labeling a diagram; discussing ailments. Teach/review names of body parts. Play a reinforcement game: Point at various parts of your body and say, "This is my (ear). This is my (foot)." Students will touch that part of their bodies and repeat after you. Occasionally name a part incorrectly (point at your knee and say, "This is my ankle.") Students should correct you: "No! This is my knee." Keep the pace lively. Have students read aloud as a group the words in Data Bank A. Teach the new words in Part B and practice pronunciation before assigning the page as independent written work.

100

A Visit to the Doctor

Look at the pictures.

A **Put the story in chronological order. The pictures and the numbers correspond. Use your dictionary if you have to.**

_____ First, the doctor examines Amy's ears, nose, and throat.

_____ Then the nurse weighs Amy. She's 121 pounds!

_____ Next, the doctor checks her back.

___1___ Every year, Amy goes to the doctor for a regular check-up.

_____ Before she leaves, Amy thanks Dr. Baker, shakes her hand, and says goodbye.

_____ When Amy arrives, she sits in the waiting room and reads a magazine.

_____ Next, the nurse takes her blood pressure. It's normal.

_____ Then the nurse calls her into the examining room.

_____ The doctor also checks her heart, lungs, and stomach.

_____ In this room, Amy takes off her clothes and puts on a hospital gown.

_____ Then the nurse takes a blood sample to do some tests.

_____ After that, Dr. Baker comes in and says hello.

B **Now write the story in paragraph form in your notebook.**

How's the Weather?

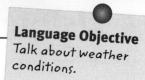

People are always talking about the weather. Read these quotations and tell what the weather is like. The first one is done for you.

1. "We can go skiing tomorrow."

   It's snowing.

2. "Look, a hat is flying down the street."

   _____

3. "I'm not taking my umbrella, but I am wearing my raincoat."

   _____

4. "The sky is gray and dark. You can't see the sun."

   _____

5. "I'm not wearing my coat today. My jacket is fine for this weather."

   _____

6. "Listen to me, Billy. You have to wear your gloves and hat and coat today."

   _____

7. "Look at the thermometer. It's 105 degrees Fahrenheit. Wow!"

   _____

8. "Oh my goodness, you are wet all over. Your shoes and socks are wet too!"

   _____

9. "The bright light hurts my eyes. I have to wear my dark glasses."

   _____

10. "We can't play baseball today. The field is wet and muddy."

    _____

DATA BANK				
cloudy	drizzling	pouring	~~snowing~~	warm
cold	hot	raining	sunny	windy

SKILL OBJECTIVES: Building vocabulary; making inferences. Teach/review the weather vocabulary in the Data Bank. Explain to students that 105 degrees Fahrenheit can be abbreviated to 105° F. Do the first one or two examples orally as a group, then assign the page for independent written work. Have students discuss their answers.

What and Why?

A Write the letter for the *Why* that goes with each *What*.
The first one is done for you.

What are they doing?		**Why are they doing it?**
1. Maria is buying two pairs of shoes.	__e__	**a.** They are married.
2. Angel is taking off his sweater.	_____	**b.** Her hands are very cold.
3. Dot is putting on her gloves.	_____	**c.** He is going out in the rain.
4. Francisco is putting on his raincoat.	_____	**d.** They are going to work.
5. The nurses are putting on their uniforms.	_____	**e.** She is at a shoe sale.
6. Loc is putting on his bathing suit.	_____	**f.** It's hot in his room.
7. James and Sandy are wearing wedding rings.	_____	**g.** He is going out in the snow.
8. Pablo is putting on his boots.	_____	**h.** He is going to the beach.

B What about you? Tell *why*. Use complete sentences. The first one is done for you.

1. You are closing the window.

   _I am closing the window because it's cold._____

2. You are wearing sunglasses.

   _____

3. You are not going to school.

   _____

4. You are calling the fire department.

   _____

5. You are crying.

   _____

6. You are cleaning your room.

   _____

7. You are studying.

   _____

DATA BANK			
today is a holiday	my room is messy	~~it's cold~~	there is a fire down the street
I have a big test tomorrow	it's very sunny outside		my best friend is moving away

SKILL OBJECTIVE: Recognizing cause and effect. On the board, write the sentence, *Paul is taking off his hat.* Ask, "Why is he taking off his hat?" Let students suggest a variety of reasons. (He is in a house/a church. It is very hot, etc.) Repeat this cause-effect activity with the sentences, *I am running* and *Her hair is wet.* Encourage students to come up with a wide range of possible causes. Do the first few examples in Parts A and B together, then assign the page as independent written work. Students may use the causes in the Data Bank for Part B or make up their own.

The Big Concert

Read the story.

Language Objective
Answer questions about a reading.

Bob is very excited. He and his friends are going to see his favorite band tonight. His friends will pick him up at 5:30. The concert starts at 8:30.

But there is a chance they will not get into the concert. Bob and his friends don't have their tickets yet. The box office opens at 6:00. They want to be among the first in line. They want to be sure they will get tickets. They don't think it's fair that the box office opens so late.

Bob's friend, Lee, had wanted to go to a movie instead. He had said it would be easier to get tickets, and it would also cost less. But everyone else wanted to go hear the band.

Bob hears the doorbell. That must be his friends. Time to go!

A **Answer the following questions. Use short answers. The first one is done for you.**

1. What time are Bob's friends coming? ___5:30___

2. Who are Bob and his friends going to hear? _____

3. When does the concert start? _____

4. Is it certain that they will get in? _____

5. When does the box office open? _____

6. Do Bob and his friends think it is fair to open the box office so late? _____

7. What did Bob's friend, Lee, want to do? _____

8. Why did he want to do that? _____

9. Did anyone agree with Lee? _____

10. What tells Bob that his friends are here? _____

B **What is the main idea of this story? Circle the answer.**

a. Bob likes hearing bands.

b. Bob is going to a concert with his friends.

c. Bob is impatient.

d. Bob does not want to be late.

C **Talk about these questions.**

1. Why isn't Bob going to the concert by himself?

2. Why is Bob so nervous?

3. Why is Lee going to the concert instead of a movie?

SKILL OBJECTIVES: Identifying main idea and details; making inferences and judgments. Read the story aloud as students follow along, or have a volunteer read it. Explain any new vocabulary. Have students reread the text silently, then answer the questions in Parts A and B. Correct Part A together. Then discuss why "going to a concert with his friends" is the only correct answer to Part B. Use the questions in Part C as springboards for class discussion.

Crossword Puzzle

Language Objective
Solve a crossword puzzle.

Write the words in the right places. Numbers 1 Across and 1 Down are done for you.

Across

1. Please _____ down.
4. Guitars make it.
7. Where you get books.
9. Person high up in a circus.
10. Where you sleep.
12. In winter, Gina _____ down the hills.
15. You eat out in them.
18. Either this _____ that.
19. What _____ of shop is it?
21. Get _____ of here.
23. New and up to date.
26. Where did she _____?
27. Jim is _____ in the gym.
30. Where you play basketball.
32. The book is _____ the table.
33. Maria is _____ the book.
34. When it is _____, everything outside is white.

Down

1. Rosa is _____ at my house.
2. Where you probably are now (if you're in school).
3. A new _____ of shoes
4. That's _____ pencil, not yours.
5. What ice cream and snow are.
6. They were _____ at pictures.
8. What is _____?
11. What happens in 15 Across.
13. Have a _____ of coffee.
14. What are you _____ about?
16. You are studying and _____ am I.
17. _____ or false?
20. Will you _____ something for me?
21. Look at that boy _____ there!
22. At that place.
24. What are you _____ tonight?
25. Yes or _____?
28. Brother of a daughter.
29. It makes the car go.
31. Was it a _____ or a woman?

(Answers are on page 119.)

Dear Dot

Language Objectives
Answer questions about a reading. Give advice. Agree or disagree with advice.

Dear Dot,
The Pattersons are coming for dinner this Sunday. I like the Pattersons, but they always talk about their health problems. They talk about their headaches and their backaches or stomach problems or sore throats. I don't like that kind of conversation, especially at the dinner table. I like to talk about movies, books, and the news. What can I do?

Healthy

1. Who is coming to dinner? _____

2. When are they coming to dinner? _____

3. What kind of health problems do they talk about? _____

_____

4. What does Healthy like to talk about? _____

_____

5. What is your advice for Healthy? Write a letter telling her what to do and what *not* to do.

Dear Healthy,

_____

_____

_____

_____

_____

_____

_____

_____

_____

SKILL OBJECTIVES: Reading comprehension; making judgments; writing a letter. Read the letter aloud las students follow along, or have a volunteer read it. Explain any unfamiliar words. Ask students to reread the letter silently, then answer questions 1–4. Discuss and correct their answers. Discuss possible answers to question 5, and then have students write their answers to Healthy.

Vocabulary Review

Complete each sentence with a word from the Data Bank.

1. My _____ name is Gonzalez.

2. Open your _____ to page twenty.

3. He is walking _____ the steps.

4. _____ I go to the bathroom, please?

5. I want to see the nurse; I feel _____.

6. Mary is _____ blue shorts and a gray blouse.

7. Every country has its own _____.

8. The bus _____ Barrington at 6:30 a.m.

9. My shoes are _____ the bed.

10. The library is _____ the bank and the post office.

11. The cat isn't chubby; she's _____.

12. Your cousin is a _____ person.

13. _____ are sweet and round.

14. Mrs. Perez is buying a _____ of milk.

15. Mr. Yu is looking for his _____.

16. Pat's _____ have blond hair.

17. Pablo is sleeping in the _____.

18. Do you live on the _____ floor?

19. A _____ types letters in an office.

20. Dinh is _____; he comes from Vietnam.

DATA BANK						
grapes	first	up	leaves	between	wife	wearing
last	thin	secretary	under	Vietnamese	sisters	May
friendly	bedroom	book	sick	flag	gallon	

VOCABULARY REVIEW. The following eight pages present a cumulative review of key vocabulary used in *Skill Sharpeners 1*. Familiar formats are used so that students can work indepedently on these pages.

Vocabulary Review

Complete each sentence with a word from the Data Bank.

1. They are _____ their car to Chicago.

2. The _____ says, "No Right Turn."

3. I have a _____ throat.

4. I am _____ tennis with my brother.

5. On _____ I'm going to the library.

6. Don't move; the photographer is taking a _____.

7. _____ your hand to answer a question.

8. Nurses take _____ of sick people.

9. Do you know your address and _____ code?

10. The _____ in the spring is rainy and warm.

11. He is _____ for fruits and vegetables.

12. _____ are many banks in this city.

13. Her first _____ is Irina.

14. A pilot flies _____.

15. _____ like to play with toys and games.

16. My birthday is on the _____ of this month.

17. Please _____ the dog if he is hungry.

18. The girls are _____ television in the living room.

19. _____ many people are in your school?

20. Jia Li's _____ is $45,000 a year.

DATA BANK						
feed	name	care	Children	driving	weather	airplanes
salary	shopping	Wednesday	sign	watching	There	picture
How	sore	Raise	tenth	playing	zip	

Vocabulary Review

Complete each sentence with a word from the Data Bank.

1. Please _____ the chalkboard.

2. Jana doesn't understand the story; she's _____.

3. I have a _____ of boots in the bedroom.

4. Four _____ equal one dollar.

5. The bus _____ at Plymouth at 4:15 p.m.

6. Most basketball players are _____.

7. I would like a chicken _____, please.

8. She's not very _____ today; she only wants a salad.

9. Carl is buying a _____ of bread at the store.

10. Susan's _____ is a nice man.

11. There are ten males and fourteen _____ in our class.

12. My keys are upstairs in Bill's _____.

13. The boys are _____ magazines in the library.

14. Yoko and her father are washing the car out in the _____.

15. The _____ look and dress the same.

16. The _____ clean the school building every day.

17. What's your _____ color?

18. My _____ hurt when I walk too much.

19. Two students are _____ in the home economics class.

20. That store is always _____ on Saturday mornings.

DATA BANK						
brother-in-law	twins	erase	hungry	custodians	cooking	sandwich
quarters	tall	females	apartment	reading	arrives	crowded
loaf	yard	favorite	confused	feet	pair	

Vocabulary Review

Complete each sentence with a word from the Data Bank.

1. Mae Lee is going to the doctor _____ work.

2. Sandra has to take care of the _____ this afternoon.

3. Clean the sink and the _____, please.

4. My girlfriend is a very _____ girl.

5. I don't know the answer to those arithmetic _____.

6. Maine is one of the New England _____.

7. Andrea is wearing her favorite _____.

8. My favorite breakfast is ham and _____.

9. The door is locked and I don't have the _____.

10. I'm not sick today; I feel _____.

11. Chess is a difficult _____ to learn.

12. I have to _____; my mother is waiting for me.

13. The boys are late; they have to _____ to school.

14. My friends are cooking dinner in the _____.

15. Please don't talk; you are in a _____.

16. Paula's _____ are in the closet.

17. The receptionists have to _____ coffee for the customers.

18. The boys are buying two rock and roll _____.

19. Maria is staying in Los Angeles for one _____.

20. It's hot in here; open the _____.

DATA BANK						
library	fine	after	pants	game	dress	baby
key	kitchen	window	go	make	beautiful	states
bathtub	week	problems	eggs	CDs	run	

Vocabulary Review

Complete each sentence with a word from the Data Bank.

1. Raul isn't walking to school today; he's taking the _____.

2. Don't touch that wall; the paint is _____.

3. I have to wear a _____; these pants are too big.

4. The teacher is _____ because the students are cheating.

5. Mrs. Pena's office is on the third floor of the Tower _____.

6. My plane is _____ soon; I have to say good-bye.

7. They drink _____ at breakfast every morning.

8. His _____ is an excellent athlete.

9. What _____ shoe are you looking for?

10. My hands are cold; where are my _____?

11. The steak is very _____ at this restaurant.

12. I am _____; may I have a drink?

13. In the winter we can _____ on this pond.

14. In the summer, _____ is everyone's favorite dessert.

15. Turn on the _____; I can't see a thing.

16. Mario is home alone; his _____ are away for the day.

17. The _____ is talking to the airport manager.

18. There are a lot of _____ in the store today.

19. I can't eat a large pizza; I want a _____ one, please.

20. I have to go to the dentist; I have a bad _____.

DATA BANK						
ice cream	tooth	coffee	bus	lamp	angry	gloves
size	pilot	daughter	belt	parents	people	expensive
thirsty	wet	Building	small	skate	leaving	

VOCABULARY REVIEW. See annotation on page 107.

Vocabulary Review

Put the words from the Data Bank into the correct boxes.

Body Parts	Fruit	Occupations
1. _____	1. _____	1. _____
2. _____	2. _____	2. _____
3. _____	3. _____	3. _____
4. _____	4. _____	4. _____
5. _____	5. _____	5. _____

Clothing	Parts of a Bicycle	Family Members
1. _____	1. _____	1. _____
2. _____	2. _____	2. _____
3. _____	3. _____	3. _____
4. _____	4. _____	4. _____
5. _____	5. _____	5. _____

Time Words	Colors
1. _____	1. _____
2. _____	2. _____
3. _____	3. _____
4. _____	4. _____
5. _____	5. _____

DATA BANK

afternoon	boots	granddaughter	night	son
ankle	chain	grapes	noon	strawberries
apple	chef	gray	pear	suit
architect	chest	handlebars	pedal	throat
aunt	coat	jeans	purple	thumb
banana	cousin	knee	red	tire
bathrobe	engineer	lawyer	seat	waitress
black	evening	morning	sister	yellow

VOCABULARY REVIEW. See annotation on page 107.

Vocabulary Review

Put the words from the Data Bank into the correct boxes.

Parts of a Car	Animals	Weather Words
1. _____	1. _____	1. _____
2. _____	2. _____	2. _____
3. _____	3. _____	3. _____
4. _____	4. _____	4. _____
5. _____	5. _____	5. _____

Furniture	Vegetables	Rooms
1. _____	1. _____	1. _____
2. _____	2. _____	2. _____
3. _____	3. _____	3. _____
4. _____	4. _____	4. _____
5. _____	5. _____	5. _____

Ordinal Numbers	Eating Utensils
1. _____	1. _____
2. _____	2. _____
3. _____	3. _____
4. _____	4. _____
5. _____	5. _____

DATA BANK

armchair	cat	elephant	kitchen	steering wheel
bathroom	cold	fifth	knife	sunny
beans	corn	first	living room	table
bed	cucumber	fork	plate	third
bedroom	cup	fourth	potatoes	tiger
bookcase	dining room	headlight	second	warm
brake pedal	dog	horse	sofa	windshield wiper
carrots	drizzling	ignition	spoon	windy

Vocabulary Review

A **Match the words in column A with their definitions in column B.**

Column A		Column B
1. astronaut	_____	**a.** street or road
2. Canadian	_____	**b.** dirty, not clean
3. restaurant	_____	**c.** place to swim
4. avenue	_____	**d.** not married
5. dialing	_____	**e.** repair, make better
6. beach	_____	**f.** doctor for animals
7. suitcase	_____	**g.** front part of neck
8. messy	_____	**h.** in back of
9. thirsty	_____	**i.** place to eat breakfast, lunch, or dinner
10. fix	_____	**j.** not rich, without money
11. throat	_____	**k.** place to wash
12. drizzling	_____	**l.** man or woman in space
13. behind	_____	**m.** school or college
14. single	_____	**n.** small animals with long tails
15. poor	_____	**o.** male child
16. son	_____	**p.** calling a phone number
17. sink	_____	**q.** raining a little
18. veterinarian	_____	**r.** person from Canada
19. university	_____	**s.** wanting a drink
20. mice	_____	**t.** kind of case for carrying clothes

B **Now show that you know what the words mean. Write a complete sentence in your notebook for each word in column A. Underline the word you are using.**

Example: *Maria is packing her <u>suitcase</u>.*

End of Book Test: Completing Familiar Structures

Circle the best answer.

Example: _____ you going to go to the bank today?

    a. Is   **b.** (Are)   **c.** Do   **d.** Can

1. Liana is here but her sisters _____.

    a. can't   **b.** isn't   **c.** don't   **d.** aren't

2. Yerik is _____.

    a. an architect   **b.** one architect   **c.** architect   **d.** architects

3. Francis is living _____ Main Street.

    a. to   **b.** at   **c.** on   **d.** for

4. My brother is listening _____ the news.

    a. to   **b.** at   **c.** on   **d.** for

5. Your socks are _____ the bed.

    a. across from   **b.** over   **c.** under   **d.** next

6. Mr. and Mrs. Jackson _____ the newspaper now.

    a. reading   **b.** read   **c.** reads   **d.** are reading

7. _____ bananas are very good.

    a. These   **b.** This   **c.** That   **d.** Them

8. _____ one hospital in Boxville.

    a. It is   **b.** There is   **c.** It has   **d.** There are

9. Juanita can swim but her brother _____.

    a. isn't   **b.** don't   **c.** doesn't   **d.** can't

10. What's the weather like today? It's _____.

    a. rain   **b.** to rain   **c.** raining   **d.** rains

11. That's Boris's coat. Please give it to _____.

    a. him   **b.** his   **c.** he   **d.** himself

12. _____ 's a sale at Lacy's Shoes today.

    a. Their   **b.** The   **c.** There   **d.** It

END OF BOOK TEST. The following testing pages will help you evaluate each student's strengths and weaknesses, and indicate his or her readiness to proceed to the next level of instruction. Review directions and examples with the class, then assign the pages as independent work. Remind students to try each answer choice in the blank space to determine which choice is correct.

End of Book Test: Completing Familiar Structures (Continued)

Circle the best answer.

13. _____ is she coming?

    a. Where **b.** When **c.** Who **d.** What

14. Why can't Paula come to class? She _____ a bad headache.

    a. has **b.** have **c.** is **d.** having

15. Our vacation is _____ August.

    a. on **b.** at **c.** for **d.** in

16. _____ are they going to do tonight?

    a. What **b.** Where **c.** What time **d.** Why

17. There's an old church _____ the library.

    a. next **b.** in front **c.** across **d.** near

18. Xiang and Jill are tired, so I am helping _____.

    a. they **b.** them **c.** there **d.** their

19. Is this your coat? No, it's _____ coat.

    a. Mary **b.** Marys **c.** hers **d.** Mary's

20. What are you _____?

    a. eat **b.** to eat **c.** eating **d.** eats

21. How much _____ those boots?

    a. are **b.** is **c.** do cost **d.** does

22. _____ umbrella is this?

    a. Who's **b.** How's **c.** What's **d.** Whose

23. How _____ airports are there in Dallas?

    a. many **b.** much **c.** are **d.** are there

24. I am looking _____ a new pair of shoes.

    a. from **b.** in **c.** for **d.** on

25. Can you help me? No, I'm sorry. I _____ go to the dentist.

    a. have **b.** am **c.** going **d.** have to

END OF BOOK TEST. See annotation on page 115.

End of Book Test: Writing Questions

Read the sentence. Write the question.

Example: Linda is taking piano lessons at the conservatory.

Where _is Linda taking piano lessons?_ _____

1. Maria is going to the library at ten o'clock.

When _____?

2. They are traveling in Central America now.

Where _____?

3. Carlotta is wearing her sister's sweater.

What _____?

4. The maid is cleaning the room.

Who _____?

5. There are four students from Vietnam in my class.

How many _____?

6. No, I'm not happy with my new apartment.

Are _____?

7. Carlos is playing volleyball in the park.

Where _____?

8. That car is $10,000.

How much _____?

9. It's going to rain tonight.

What _____?

10. She's crying because she is sad.

Why _____?

11. I'm wearing my brother's sneakers.

Whose _____?

12. No, Nancy's mother is an engineer.

Is _____?

END OF BOOK TEST. Go over the directions and example with the class. Point out that the first word(s) of each question is/are provided. Assign the page as independent written work.

End of Book Test: Reading for Details

Read the story.

The Play

Mr. Hawker's class is on their way back to school. They have just been to see a play at a local theater. There were students from other schools seeing the play, too.

The play was supposed to be a comedy. A comedy is a play that is meant to make you laugh. Most comedies have happy endings.

The play was two hours long. It was about a teacher who has a very mischievous class. His students are always getting into trouble. They play tricks on the teacher. They make fun of him when his back is turned. This class is not like Mr. Hawker's class. Mr. Hawker's students behave themselves.

The teacher in the play finally figures out a way to make his class quieter. He reads them a funny story. The story is about a class just like theirs! His class then learns that they are the silly ones, not the teacher.

Most people in Mr. Hawker's class said they liked the play. Jin and Sara did not. They thought it was boring, and it didn't get many laughs.

Answer the following questions.

1. Where is Mr. Hawker's class going? _____

2. Where has Mr. Hawker's class been? _____

3. What is a comedy? _____

4. How long was the play? _____

5. How do the students in the play get into trouble? _____

6. How does Mr. Hawker's class act? _____

7. How does the teacher in the play solve the problem? _____

8. What did the teacher's class learn? _____

9. What did most of Mr. Hawker's class think of the play? _____

10. What did Jin and Sara think of the play? _____

END OF BOOK TEST. Students should read this story several times, then answer the comprehension questions. Accept factually correct short answers as well as complete sentences.

118

Sample Paragraph

Use this as a sample of the way to write a paragraph.

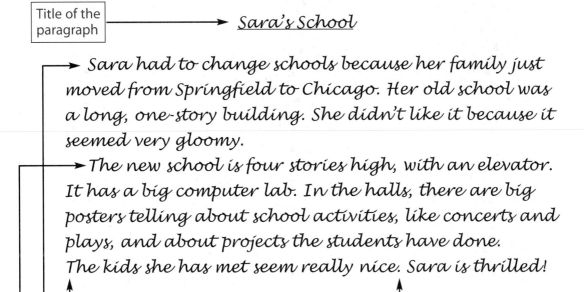

Title of the paragraph ⟶ _Sara's School_

Sara had to change schools because her family just moved from Springfield to Chicago. Her old school was a long, one-story building. She didn't like it because it seemed very gloomy.

The new school is four stories high, with an elevator. It has a big computer lab. In the halls, there are big posters telling about school activities, like concerts and plays, and about projects the students have done. The kids she has met seem really nice. Sara is thrilled!

All sentences begin with a capital letter.

All sentences end with a period.

The first word in a paragraph is indented; that is, it starts a few spaces in from the margin.

Each paragraph starts on a new line.

Answers to puzzle on page 105.

SAMPLE PARAGRAPH. Use this page as a sample for the task of writing a paragraph. References are made to it on many pages that include instructions to write paragraphs. You may wish to point out that not all paragraphs require titles, and that all should contain a topic sentence; this is usually, but not always, the first sentence in the paragraph.

Index of Language Objectives